Theatre and the Threshold of Death

Thinking through Theatre seeks to advance theatre and performance studies by exploring the questions performance itself is uniquely capable of asking, and by interrogating the ways in which it asks them. The series seeks to problematize the distinction between "making" and "thinking" by stressing their inter-relation and by identifying in theatre and performance practices aesthetic and political forms of thought and action.

The *Thinking through Theatre* series aims to examine theatre and performance practices as material forms of thought, and to articulate the knowledge embedded within them. The series examines the ways in which theatre is continually rethinking the possibilities of movement, space, action, image, voice, etc., exploring the logics of creative invention and critical investigation that enable performance to operate as a mode of thought *sui generis*.

Series Editors

Maaike Bleeker (Utrecht University, Netherlands), Adrian Kear (Wimbledon College of Arts, University of the Arts, London, UK), JoeKelleher (University of Roehampton, London, UK) and Heike Roms (University of Exeter, UK)

Published Titles

Thinking through Theatre and Performance edited by Maaike Bleeker, Adrian Kear, Joe Kelleher and Heike Roms

Nomadic Theatre: Mobilizing Theory and Practice on the European Stage by Liesbeth Groot Nibbelink

Rethinking Roland Barthes through Performance: A Desire for Neutral Dramaturgy edited by Harry Robert Wilson and Will Daddario

Forthcoming titles

In Solitude: The Philosophy of Digital Performance Encounters by Eirini Nedelkopoulou

Performance Criticism as Political Event: Nonconforming Practices and Covert Poetics by Diana Damian Martin

Theatres of Powerlessness: Acts of Knowledge and the Performance of the Many edited by Edit Kaldor and Joe Kelleher

Theatre and the Threshold of Death

Lectures on the Dying Arts

Kathleen M. Gough

methuen | drama
LONDON • NEW YORK • OXFORD • NEW DELHI • SYDNEY

METHUEN DRAMA
Bloomsbury Publishing Plc, 50 Bedford Square, London, WC1B 3DP, UK
Bloomsbury Publishing Inc, 1385 Broadway, New York, NY 10018, USA
Bloomsbury Publishing Ireland, 29 Earlsfort Terrace, Dublin 2, D02 AY28, Ireland

BLOOMSBURY, METHUEN DRAMA and the Methuen Drama logo are
trademarks of Bloomsbury Publishing Plc

First published in Great Britain 2024
Paperback edition published 2025

Copyright © Kathleen M. Gough, 2024

Kathleen M. Gough has asserted her right under the Copyright, Designs and
Patents Act, 1988, to be identified as author of this work.

For legal purposes the Acknowledgments on pp. xii–xiii constitute an
extension of this copyright page.

Cover design: Ben Anslow

All rights reserved. No part of this publication may be: i) reproduced or transmitted in any
form, electronic or mechanical, including photocopying, recording or by means of
any information storage or retrieval system without prior permission in writing from
the publishers; or ii) used or reproduced in any way for the training, development or
operation of artificial intelligence (AI) technologies, including generative AI technologies.
The rights holders expressly reserve this publication from the text and data mining
exception as per Article 4(3) of the Digital Single Market Directive (EU) 2019/790.

Bloomsbury Publishing Plc does not have any control over, or responsibility for,
any third-party websites referred to or in this book. All internet addresses given
in this book were correct at the time of going to press. The author and publisher
regret any inconvenience caused if addresses have changed or sites have ceased
to exist, but can accept no responsibility for any such changes.

A catalogue record for this book is available from the British Library.

A catalog record for this book is available from the Library of Congress.

Library of Congress Cataloging-in-Publication Data

Names: Gough, Kathleen M., 1972- author.
Title: Theatre and the threshold of death : lectures on the dying arts / Kathleen M. Gough.
Description: London ; New York : Methuen Drama, 2024. | Series: Thinking
through theatre | Includes bibliographical references and index.
Identifiers: LCCN 2023025275 (print) | LCCN 2023025276 (ebook) |
ISBN 9781350385511 (hardback) | ISBN 9781350385566 (paperback) |
ISBN 9781350385528 (pdf) | ISBN 9781350385535 (epub)
Subjects: LCSH: Mysteries and miracle-plays–History and criticism. |
Religious drama–History and criticism. | Liminality in literature. |
Life cycle, Human, in literature. | Theater–Philosophy. | LCGFT: Lectures.
Classification: LCC PN1761 .G68 2024 (print) | LCC PN1761 (ebook) |
DDC 809.2/516–dc23/eng/20230920
LC record available at https://lccn.loc.gov/2023025275
LC ebook record available at https://lccn.loc.gov/2023025276

ISBN: HB: 978-1-3503-8551-1
PB: 978-1-3503-8556-6
ePDF: 978-1-3503-8552-8
eBook: 978-1-3503-8553-5

Series: Thinking through Theatre

Typeset by Newgen KnowledgeWorks Pvt. Ltd., Chennai, India

For product safety related questions contact productsafety@bloomsbury.com.

To find out more about our authors and books visit www.bloomsbury.com
and sign up for our newsletters.

To all my teachers and my teachers' teachers

Contents

List of Figures	x
Acknowledgments	xii
Introduction: A Visit to a Tomb	1
Lecture 1: Character Study	29
Lecture 2: Genre	47
Lecture 3: Gesture	61
Lecture 4: Alienation	81
Lecture 5: On Acting and Not Acting	97
Lecture 6: The Theatre and Its Double	117
Lecture 7: *Duende*, or Play and Death	131
Lecture 8: *Theatron*, the Seeing Place	149
References	159
Index	169

Figures

I.1. Guidonian Hand with solmization syllables, *c.* sixteenth century. Courtesy of Fine Art Images/Heritage Images/ Getty Images.   17
1.1. Illumination from Hildegard's *Scivias* depicting her receiving a vision and dictating the message to Volmar, her male secretary, 1151.   36
2.1. Giotto di Bondone, *Scenes from the Life of Mary Magdalen: Noli me tangere*, Fresco, Magdalen Chapel, Lower Church, San Francesco, Assisi, Italy, *c.* 1320s.   53
2.2. Lehman Master, *Noli me tangere*, *c.* fourteenth century. Courtesy of Universal History Archive/Universal Images Group via Getty Images.   54
2.3. Fra Angelica, *Noli me tangere*, fresco on the wall of Cell 1 of the Convento di San Marco, Florence, Italy, *c.* 1440–2.   55
2.4. Tibetan thangka painting of Green Tara, *c.* thirteenth century.   56
2.5. Painted banner (thangka) with the Medicine Buddha (Bhaishajyaguru), *c.* 1201–1400. Kate S. Buckingham Fund, Art Institute of Chicago.   57
3.1. Photograph of plaster cast of Eleonora Duse's right hand taken by author.   64
3.2. Giotto di Bondone, *Lamentation (The Mourning of Christ)*, Scrovegni Chapel, Padua, Italy, *c.* 1304–6.   71
3.3. Duccio, *Descent from the Cross*, Museo dell'Opera del Duomo, Siena, Italy, *c.* 1308–11.   72
3.4. Film still of Eleonora Duse playing Rosalia Derios in *Cenere*, dir. Fabo Mari, Ambrosio Film Company, Italy, 1916.   73

5.1. Marina Abramović, *Rhythm 10*, Performance, 1 Hour, Museo d'Arte Contemporanea Villa Borghese, Rome, Italy, 1973. © Marina Abramović, Courtesy of the Marina Abramović Archives. 110
6.1. Caravaggio, *The Incredulity of Saint Thomas*, Florence, Italy, 1601. 126
7.1. An employee poses with a series entitled *The Ten Largest* (1907). L–R: No. 6, Adulthood; No. 7, Adulthood; No. 8, Adulthood; and No. 10, Old Age by Hilma af Klint as part of the Serpentine Galleries' Spring Exhibition in central London on March 2, 2016. Photo credit Ben Stansall/AFP via Getty Images. 136

Acknowledgments

There are many institutions and people I wish to thank for this book coming into the world. My sincere thanks to the University of Glasgow Archives which houses the Eleonora Duse Special Collection; the Live Art Development Agency (LADA) in London; Arthur Findlay College in Stansted Mountfitchet; Kathleen Scacciaferro, Healing Touch teacher in the Nursing Program at the University of Vermont (UVM); Francesca Arnoldy, founder and former principal teacher of the End-of-Life Doula Certificate Program in the Larner College of Medicine at UVM; Nicole Dupont, former Hospice Volunteer Coordinator in Central Vermont; Omega Institute in Rhinebeck, NY; Monastery of the Immaculate Heart of Mary in Westfield, Vermont; The Golden Sufi Center in Northern California; and Dhamma Dhara Vipassana Meditation Center in Shelburne, Massachusetts. The experiences I had in the archives, programs, seminars, courses, hospice care settings, and spiritual institutions were paradigm shifting.

I also wish to thank the UVM Humanities Center where I was a Faculty Fellow in 2021–22, the UVM Contemplative Faculty Learning Community where I was a fellow in 2020–21, the UVM College of Arts & Sciences for a Small Grant Research Award, and the UVM Office of the Vice President for Research for an Express Award. My gratitude extends to Daniel Sack for permission to reprint a small selection of prose first published in *Imagined Theatres* as "The Age of Duse: Notes for a Performative Lecture" (Summer 2020). In addition, the epigraph in the introduction from *Waiting for Godot* by Samuel Beckett is reprinted with the permission of Faber & Faber Ltd. In North America, *Waiting for Godot* copyright © 1954 is reprinted with the permission of Grove Press, Inc.; Copyright © renewal 1982 by Samuel Beckett. Used by permission of Grove/Atlantic, Inc.

Any third-party use of this material, outside of this publication, is prohibited. Lastly, all extracts from scripture are taken from the Holy Bible, New International Version. Copyright 1973, 1978, 1984 Biblica. All rights reserved throughout the world. Used by permission of Biblica.

In the years spent working on this project, love and mystery have been ongoing themes to conversations with dear friends: Renu Cappelli, Will Daddario, Vijay Kanagala, Louise Todd, Sharon Ultsch, Joanne Zerdy, and with my wise partner, Rick Eschholz. They are also the topics of conversation I continue to have with myself, my students, and the artists I write about in these pages: Hildegard of Bingen, Eleonora Duse, Simone Weil, Marina Abramović, and Hilma af Klint.

In the first lecture in the series, I ask the question, *what is the dream of the writer?* The lectures are ultimately about how we relate to each other, and how we stay in relationship with the known and unknown world. The artists-mystics who reached out to me in some inexplicable and undeniable way went so far into their own disciplines that they broke them open only to discover that what resides at the center is ultimately their own heart—a heart that is paradoxically less personal, more malleable, and in every way shareable. If there is a dream for this writer, it is that our education might lead to wisdom, might wake us up from the trance of separation, and might allow our very questions to build worlds inside the one we think we know until the place our education leads us is, indeed, *higher, and higher, and higher.*

Introduction: A Visit to a Tomb

> Have you not done tormenting me with your accursed time! It's abominable! When! When! One day, is that not enough for you, one day he went dumb, one day I went blind, one day we'll go deaf, one day we were born and one day we shall die, the same day, the same second, is that not enough for you? (*Calmer*). They give birth astride a grave, the light gleams an instant, then it's night once more.
>
> —Beckett, *Waiting for Godot* (1954)

The rebirth of theatre in the Middle Ages begins with a visit to a tomb. When theatre begins again around AD 900, it appears in the middle of the Christian Mass and recounts the musical mystery of Jesus's missing body, a dematerialized body, a body presumed dead, a body that the three Marys who visit the tomb assume will be a corpse. *Visitatio Sepulchri* (Latin for "a visit to the tomb"), now considered the first mystery play,[1] is the sung trope in the Easter Mass that not only tells the story of the missing corpse, but according to the Angel waiting outside the tomb who speaks to the three Marys, the story of Jesus rising from the dead. Death, it is implied, is not what we think it is.

That the rebirth of theatre begins with the story of a missing body who is alive in another way, but a way no less fleshy, is instructive. That theatre's mysterious return in the Middle Ages appears in the middle of the Christian Mass to tell the story of a man who is in the middle of death and a new life also puts us squarely in the middle, where death is not an ending, but appears as a threshold, a doorway—something that requires our curiosity, something that we cannot actually know with any certainty, something that asks us to engage our imagination, something that sounds remarkably like theatre.

The other name for this seedling drama that appears in the middle of the Easter Mass is *Quem quaeritis* (Latin for "whom do you seek?"), which is the question the Angel asks of the three Marys as they journey toward Jesus's tomb: Whom do you seek in the sepulchre? In this brief call and response playlet—four lines of plainchant—we get many of the significant elements of theatrical storytelling: characters, journey, discovery, revelation.[2]

I had the opportunity to journey to an ancient tomb recently, and in some oblique way, I was also seeking a re(ve)lation. Maeshowe, a Neolithic burial chamber located on the mainland of the Orkney Islands off the northeast coast of Scotland, is roughly three thousand years older than the tomb the Marys visit, and three thousand miles north of Jerusalem. As such it is less dusty cave and more damp-and-grassy mound. Looking at drone images, you would not be mistaken for thinking that the site was not an ancient burial mound, but a prototype for a future ship to take you inside Mother Earth. Considered the finest chambered tomb in northwest Europe, it rests at the center of a larger ceremonial landscape with standing stones scattered in the distance and the substantial Ring of Brodgar down the street. However, the original function of Maeshowe remains a bit of a mystery.

One of the foremost extraordinary facts about this burial chamber is the simple reality that it is still intact five thousand years after its creation despite being on an island with an inhospitable climate due largely to its location at the intersection of where the Atlantic Ocean meets the North Sea. Another rather surprising fact is that it holds one of the largest collections of Norse runes in the world. Shortly after Christmas in 1153, when Earl Harald Maddadarson (Orkney was part of Norway until 1468) was traveling with his men, they were stranded by a snowstorm and took shelter in Maeshowe. Perhaps trying to pass the time, they wrote rune messages on the walls of the chamber that are still intact, most of which announce that such-and-such was "here."³ Maeshowe was next rediscovered by the Victorians, who went in through the roof since the large stone at the entryway could not be moved. Curiously, there were only two or three bones discovered in the tomb (and one of those was of a horse). There is some speculation as to its use as a burial chamber at all. It is agreed, however, that it was entered regularly by the living, most likely to perform ceremonies on behalf of the wider community.

When visiting a tomb, one is typically looking for a relation—a friend, or family member, or exalted teacher. But what if when you visit a tomb, the relation you are seeking feels more mysterious? After all, the relation the Marys think they are seeking at the tomb is ultimately unknown to them, a relation that up until that moment was not thinkable. Did this new relation then change their relation to their own finitude, their own sense of self? Walking toward the Maeshowe burial chamber on a damp October day, I heard a voice that did not sound like my own tell me, "There's something for you here." I blinked, looked around, and then heard it again.

To get inside the burial chamber you must pass through a narrow entranceway that is just over a meter high and eleven meters long. Once you have walk-crawled through this passage, you come to a surprisingly large, dark, circular space where the air moves differently, and the outside world feels like another planet. Perhaps it was the feeling that I was walking back up a birth canal and into a womb that made me pay such close attention to my body, the bodies around me, and the bodies who have stood there before me, or, who, like the runes suggest, are still "here." This womb-like burial chamber was a threshold that brought the Neolithic world, the Norse world, the Victorian world, and my world into relation. It did so through a cyclical performance that Earl Harald Maddadarson and his men may have witnessed in the days around Christmas in 1153.

For about two weeks, on either side of the winter solstice, when the sun is low in the sky (if there is sun), it cuts through the center of a standing stone called the Barnhouse stone, a half mile away from Maeshowe. From there, the sun's rays move across the sky and shine straight down the low and narrow entryway into the burial chamber where the pitch-black interior is illuminated. I did not visit on the solstice, but I have seen photographs. It is an awe-inspiring performance—an incredible feat of engineering that brings all of life's cycles into relation.

In the year leading up to my visit to the tomb, I had lost some fundamental relationship to the world. I often felt I was walking dead, a corpse, unmoored from the world around me. The revelation of this cyclical performance woke up some part of me that was just becoming conscious—an aspect that embodied a sense of wonder as if for the first time. I was not dead, and my body was not missing. It was right here, passing through one of life's cycles. At the death of the year comes the arrival of the sun. Three thousand years later, at the death of the year comes the arrival of the *Son*. "The torch is plucked from the dying hands of the year: and a new time has begun," writes George MacKay Brown, Orkney's beloved poet (1989: 75). For our Neolithic ancestors, our Christian ancestors, and our many other ancestors in between and adjacent down to the present moment, birth always happens astride a grave.

***

"The past is a relation," writes Rebecca Schneider (2018: 288) in her essay, "That the Past May Yet Have Another Future." In my work as a dramaturge, I am always looking for patterns, ways of seeking out relations from the past to fashion new relations in the present. I also listen deeply to the gaps in a story to hear what is not being said. Silence is also a pattern of relationship. As I began to journey toward the apex of middle age and started to get obsessed with the

Middle Ages, I paid attention to the way that my life patterns were aligning with the patterns of the first medieval mystery play—the curious way that theatre was *producing* my social reality instead of the other way around. The original notion of mystery connotes the idea of something with a hidden, mystical significance. Since the world kept offering itself to me in the form of a medieval mystery play, I decided to step inside its form—to be more conscious of its patterns, the lacunae in my own story, and the reason why the major motifs and themes influencing my life had all the trappings of (the) Middle Age(s). In fact, I had very little choice but to do so.

My mystery unfolded over several years as a variety of artists, all of whom are also considered mystics, started calling out for my attention, continually gesturing for me to follow them into unknown territory. I did not have a past relationship with these women. They were not part of my research history, nor did I find myself drawn to them in ways I could understand at the time. As my students might say, these women were not "relatable" to me. I first heard from the twelfth-century medieval mystic Hildegard of Bingen (1098–1179), considered the first known musical composer, who was also a Benedictine nun, healer, visionary, and dramatist. This was followed by a call from the world-famous fin de siècle actress, Eleonora Duse (1858–1924). Regarded as the first modern actor in the Western world, she was also hailed as a "mystic in the theatre," and was a regular meditator. The mid-twentieth-century philosopher, activist, and mystic Simone Weil (1909–1943), who Albert Camus called "the only great spirit of our time," arrived by way of the Porziuncola in Assisi where we both experienced a transformation of sorts. At around the same time, I kept bumping into the work of "the grandmother of performance art," Marina Abramović (b. 1946), whose own practice of repeating patterns of behavior followed by a career of listening in silence called out to me in some nonlinear way. Finally, Swedish artist and medium Hilma af Klint (1862–1944), the first known (and belatedly acknowledged) abstract painter, arrived by way of a dream and took me to places I had not yet imagined.

I had no idea what to do with this series of five singular figures, all of whom are a "first" in their discipline. For reasons that are unclear to me, not one of them would leave me alone. Despite my emphatic resistance, they demanded that I form some sort of relationship. Over time I started thinking of them as a kind of hierophantic faculty in an esoteric mystery school. They were certainly my teachers, but what was their teaching? After their biographical and autobiographical writing revealed little of the patterns to which I could relate, I started listening attentively for the lacuna in each of their life stories. I noticed where their stories break down, where their masks begin to slip, where they must let go of one world to make space for another, and where the thing that becomes interesting about them is the way they lose their discipline.

These creative explorers went so deep into their own discipline that they broke something open, revealing that their disciplines were like window dressing behind which appeared a world more malleable, paradoxically less personal, and more relational. I was profoundly curious about this gap, so I kept hanging out in the lacuna of their stories to see what I might learn in this liminal space between the known and unknown worlds. Remarkably, it was in this space that I started to take on the characteristics of a protagonist in a mystery play—a play that was now producing my social reality. Which is to say that once I discovered the pattern they shared, I started to lose my own discipline.

***

In 2018–19, I was fortunate to take a sabbatical from the Department of Theatre at the University of Vermont (UVM). I decided that my sabbatical task would be to say "yes" to wherever my intuition told me to go as I embarked on my research into each woman in the series. As I traveled across large distances to find them, their lives crisscrossed backward and forward in time and their stories braided their way into my own experiences. Without quite knowing why or how, each time I crossed a threshold into their world, I was—quite literally—taken to practices (courses, seminars, workshops, conferences) that were simultaneously about dying and about healing. It was such a startling and often uncomfortable experience that all-year I felt that I was being led to my own death, but it was too late: I had already said "yes."

In the autumn term of my sabbatical, I went looking for Hildegard of Bingen at a cloistered Benedictine convent on the Vermont–Québec border, and then met up with her again in a sound healing course held in a yurt in rural Vermont the following summer. My introduction to Eleonora Duse began several years ago on a ten-day silent meditation retreat before I was directed to her archive at the University of Glasgow where I discovered her famous hands, and the plaster casts made of them. I picked up her trail again in 2018 as I followed her to an Afterlife Awareness Conference in Orlando, Florida (of all places), before we were reunited in a course on Healing Touch run through the Nursing program at UVM. Simone Weil appeared quite out of the blue, but when she did her life was a revelation. My preoccupation with her death first led to my certification as an end-of-life doula through the Larner College of Medicine at UVM before training and working as a hospice volunteer in Central Vermont. I got to know Marina Abramović more intimately at the Live Art Development Agency in London, while studying her "Relation Works" (1976–88), before meeting up with her again at a family constellation workshop on transgenerational trauma and healing at the Omega Institute in New York later the same year. Finally, after Hilma af Klint found me in a dream, she sent me to the Arthur Findlay College of Psychic and Mediumship Studies on the outskirts of London before sending me to her retrospective at the Guggenheim Museum, where her largely unknown past was experiencing a different future in the aptly titled, *Hilma af Klint: Paintings for the Future.*

What was happening here? Was it personal? Surely it must be, but it didn't *feel* personal. Wasn't this about their lives? They brought me into a gap in their stories only to reveal that I had entered the gap in my own. The boundaries were so porous that I could no longer tell where their stories ended and mine began. Yet, this very challenge of separating myself from these teachers alerted me to another clue about the strangely medieval resonance of my mystery play. In Barbara Newman's *The Permeable Self: Five Medieval Relationships* (2021), she describes the concept of personhood in the medieval world as one that is counter to our understanding of "individuals in their solitude." Personhood was always interpersonal, illuminating "relations at a certain pitch of intensity, where the boundaries between persons seem to blur" (2021: 1). Crucially, "the permeable self appears most often at the liminal junctures and imagined end points of personal history" (2021: 8). "The essence of personhood," writes Newman, "is the capacity to be permeated by other selves, other persons, without being fractured by them." In this sense, "a 'person' has little to do with either the self-sufficient, much-maligned Enlightenment self or the decentered fragmented postmodern self. Rather, the personal is, by definition, the interpersonal. One cannot be a person by oneself, only with, through, and in other persons" (2021: 6).

Given how mysteriously my own play was unfolding, I should not have been surprised that the first of the five medieval relationships that she explores is the one between teacher and student. "Unlike the relationship between instructor and students in our universities," Newman writes, "the medieval bond was more like that of master and disciple in a wisdom tradition, where the student aspires to model his deepest self on the master" (2021: 9). What is more, "[m]edieval pedagogy carried this principle even further: not only the living teacher but also the long-dead author of a living text can indwell the student's mind" (2021: 10). In the liminal space that held open for me the possibility of relationship at the limits of personal history, in this space where I was "indwelling" with, through, and in other persons, was I being instructed on how to be a wholly different *kind* of person? A stereophonic kind of person? What kind of instructions might a stereophonic person require when they are thinking with, in, and through a series of teachers who, in serial installments, send them to practices where being in a healing relationship to other bodies is a fundamental requirement?

***

The lecture series that follows, *The Dying Arts*, is all about relational thinking and relational practice. It never leaves the arena of relationship. Death, itself, is a permeable relationship. Read through the discipline of theatre and performance studies, death is always in relation to "liveness," and always a relation to the living. Mark Robson, in the aptly titled *Theatre & Death* (2019), takes as his main argument that his book is inevitably "about theatre and life" (2019: ix). There are, however, a remarkable number of differences in how death is theorized both within the field and in death studies more generally. "There are some common-sense assumptions, but few stand much scrutiny once you get beyond medico-biological definitions that seem a little, well, bloodless. So many ways to begin talking about the end" (2019: ix). As Robson suggests, even in the world of medicine there is not consensus. The most recent online edition of the *Encyclopedia Britannica* "refers to multiple definitions of death, in line with modern scientific understanding of *death as a process*" (my emphasis; Curtin 2019: 12). In *Death in Modern Theatre*, Adrian Curtin writes that "recognizing the variety of ways death has been conceived and rationalized (or not) throughout history, means recognizing it as constructed nature. Death is a reality, of course, but, in a way, it is also a fiction, in that it is creatively (re)interpreted" (2019: 15). Theatre, too, is both a material reality and a fiction that is constantly reinterpreted. It is reasonable, then, that both Robson and Curtin consider theatre the interpretive *arena* where we investigate death and its theatrical representations across space and time. In these models, death may be uncertain, but it is assumed that we know what we mean by theatre. Other scholars in the field theorize one term *through* the other, forming a series of analogies that trouble the very categories they seek to explore. One creative way of thinking death through theatre and theatre through death takes place in Mischa Twitchin's *Theater of Death: The Uncanny in Mimesis*. Unpacking the analogy in his title, he writes, "theatre is to the uncanny as death is to mimesis; and (or) theatre is to mimesis as death is to the uncanny. The relation between death and theatre, as that between the uncanny and mimesis, concerns human appearances staged, across a threshold, by the living" (2016: 17). Rebecca Schneider, reflecting on what might remain after a performance has disappeared, turns to death to think through impermanence and remains. "Death appears to result in a paradoxical production of both disappearance and remains," writes Schneider. "Disappearance, that citational practice, that after-the-factness, clings to remains—absent flesh *does* ghost bones (2011: 102).

Instead of using theatre as an arena to explore death or thinking theatre *through* death and thinking death *through* theatre, I retool theatrical concepts in order that we might find ways to be *with* death by being with dying; in turn, I imagine a different way to be *with* theatre. This approach was born from my reading and training as an end-of-life doula and hospice volunteer. In those contexts, you companion someone on their journey. Your job is not to fix (the person, meaning, a situation), but to sit *with* someone in the question. If death is not something we can know with any certainty, then maybe theatre isn't either. Joan Halifax, a Zen teacher who has worked with the dying for several decades, reflects on how when we encounter death, we're called into a realm of what Buddhists refer to as "not knowing" or "beginner's mind" (2009: 1). "In being with dying," she continues, "we will encounter this not-knowing no matter how we try to map everything out or control it." Reflecting further, she writes, "This first tenet, not knowing, may seem strange to us. Conceptual knowledge is so valued in our world. Yet in many cultures, wisdom is equated not with knowledge but with an open heart. And how can we know what will happen in the next moment anyway?" (2009: 1).

Relating to change, to the unknown, to the terrifying, to pain, to the absolute, to the mysterious, to the irrational, to the paradoxical, to the awe-inspiring starts with relating to where we find these experiences in our own permeable self, our own permeable relationship with finitude. Death, in the form of impermanence, is at the center of all our relating. The inevitability of death is like gravity: whether it is acknowledged or not, it grounds you in your body. What if we move closer to our embodied experience? What if we investigate it even when—and maybe crucially when—it doesn't feel comfortable, or familiar, or "relatable"? How might this allow us to think through our own permeability with the unknown in us, and through us, the world? How might this full-bodied attention be a healing?

Considering my own embodied experiences—which most often required me to be in physical contact with other students in the courses, seminars, and workshops, and later in hospice settings—I started wondering about the relationship between education and healing.[4] My own academic training places a very different value on knowledge gained through personal experience, much less knowledge produced from touch and contact with others. So much of my life in education, and in the educational experiences of many of my students, indicates that the way we relate to our education is more often through the pedagogical harm administered by teachers (and administrators) who instruct us in how to dismiss the reality of our own experience. "If the intent of inquiry is to create a different world, to ask what kinds of futures are imaginable," writes Springgay and Truman, "then (in) tensions attend to the immersion, tension, friction, anxiety, strain, and quivering unease of doing research differently" (2018: 204). Learning to reimagine our education as an embodied experience may help to heal what is broken, which is always our relationship with the world.

This book performs in the liminal space between skepticism and knowledge and suggests that we approach the epistemology of doubt by questioning markers of validation itself, and by questioning how we measure what is valued. "Scepticism not only questions the reliability of the sense of touch as a tool to test what we can know," writes Rachel Aumiller (2021: 10). "It equally investigates how haptic encounters—experiences of coming into touch with other people, things, or ourselves—can cause us to radically question what we believe to be true" (2021: 10). That my research on artist-mystics would direct me to courses, seminars, and workshops on the topics of death, dying, and healing on the eve of a global pandemic radically shifted my relationship with the reality of my own experience.

The Dying Arts rehearses the pedagogic scene(s) through which the project is forged. The lectures are written for a course that is never taught because the discipline in which the lectures might be delivered does not exist. And yet, this thinking through *how* theatre means and *where* it can take us has the potential to open new connections and pathways for artists, students, educators, and other world builders. In this regard, it borrows from Nicholas Bourriaud's concept of relational art that "takes as its theoretical horizon the realm of human interactions and its social context, rather than the assertion of an independent and private symbolic space" (2002: 5). While Bourriaud is discussing contemporary art practice and the relationship between artistic work and the spectator, his theorizing has larger pedagogical implications. He writes that "it is no longer possible to regard the contemporary work as a space to be walked through …It is henceforth presented as a period of time to be lived through, like an opening to unlimited discussion" (2002: 5). A primary argument that flows through each of the lectures in the series is that it is essential to remain curious about our multiple and contradictory encounters with the unknown—in ourselves, in the Other, and in the world. It is the *questions* that yield insight well beyond the limitations of concretizing their potential by turning toward quick answers. Too often, thinking we have arrived at the "answer," thinking that we *know*, is the precise moment when we stop relating.

The lectures are always asking questions, always at the breaking point, always wanting to take the writer and the reader further and further away from certainty. In this way, the lectures also make an argument for the centrality of process—not simply as the means to an end, but as the end as well. Our ending is also a process. Each of the eight lectures builds on the previous and uses the conceit of the medieval mystery play as the dramaturgical framework and affect in which the writer is moving. The title of each lecture appears *as if* it is a well-rehearsed keyword or phrase in the field of theater and performance studies. However, the keywords are turned inside-out—instead of helping to unpack stage practices, the terms and phrases stumble off the stage and help us to understand end-of-life practices in the multiple ways that this is addressed. Each of the title's keywords also serve as linking terms that lead from one lecture to the next in a carefully ordered serial fashion.

***

Using the form of a lecture *series* reflects the method that I am developing. Thinking in a series is always about thinking in multiples. You are never solo, never alone, you are always in relation. Since my aim is to demonstrate how paying close attention to artistic process—our own and those with whom we are in dialogue—transforms the very destination of where disciplinary training may lead us, it is necessary to *show* this process instead of simply discussing it in a traditional narrative form. Arts researchers Springgay and Truman refer to this as "research-creation," which they describe as "the complex intersection of art practice, theoretical concepts, and research. It is an experimental practice that cannot be predicted or determined in advance. It is trans-disciplinary ... and is used by scholars attuned to the role of the arts and creativity in their own areas of expertise" ("Research-Creation," n.d.).

What does it mean and in what ways is it meaningful to think in a series? Seriality is a flexible, elastic concept. Some of the most incisive theorizing about the form comes from art historians, critics, and artists who work in series. Katharina Sykora writes that serial art is "characterized by the nonhierarchical juxtaposition of equivalent representations, which only yield their complete meaning on the basis of their mutual relationship" (1983: 7). Her concise understanding that seriality generates meaning through the juxtaposition of mutual relationships helps to contextualize Mel Bochner's influential articulation that "serial order is a method, not a style" (1967: 28). In *Serial Imagery*, John Coplans writes that "[s]eriality is identified by a particular inter-relationship, rigorously consistent, of structure and syntax: Serial structures are produced by a single indivisible process that links the internal structure of a work to that of other works within a differentiated whole" (1968: 11). According to Sol LeWitt, this method of "using a simple form repeatedly narrows the field of the work and concentrates the intensity to the arrangement of the form. This arrangement becomes the end while the form becomes the means" (1967: 80).

A less abstract and more embodied way of understanding the opportunities of working in a series (where "the arrangement becomes the end while the form becomes the means") is found in a discipline that places relationality at the center of the practice: yoga asana, which means physical yoga poses or yoga postures. To echo Bochner and LeWitt, moving from pose to pose is a method, not a style. Vinyasa krama, "wise progression," is the practice of sequencing shapes and poses. It is the method yoga teachers use to create a sequence that allows the body to move with ease from one pose to the next in the series. Peter Nelson, writing about seriality in music, clarifies that while a "series is pure succession: this, then this, then this ... each new element establishes its equality with the preceding item; its democratic right to be taken seriously as a member" (Nelson 2011: 19).

The serial method that is practiced across artistic disciplines—one that thinks through the democracy of relationships as a relation among equals—is also a teaching method. "The *Yoga Sutra* says that each person gets different things from the same teaching based on his or her [or their] own perspective. There is nothing wrong with this. This is how it is" (Desikachar 1995: xxvi). LeWitt makes a similar claim for serial art practice when he writes that "[i]t doesn't really matter if the viewer understands the concepts of the artist by seeing the art. Once out of his hand the artist has no control over the way a viewer will perceive the work. Different people will understand the same thing in a different way" (1967: 80).

In these contexts, a teaching is not something you are given but is something that you make through the ways that you relate. This lecture series is such a teaching—a way of opening a series of pathways and connections initiated by my taking seriously the nonlinear, almost musical call and response relationship between my reaching middle age and becoming obsessed with the rebirth of theatre in the Middle Ages.

***

In James Hillman's illuminating study, *Healing Fiction* (1998), he asks and answers the question: "What does historicizing do for the soul [i.e., mind, psyche]?" Hillman writes that "[h]istoricizing puts events into another genre. Neither here and now, nor once upon a time, but halfway between. Yet this between has a precise locus in history and an event placed there may require treatment in the style of that historical time" (1998: 43–4). Once I stepped into the dramaturgical form of the medieval mystery play as a way of orienting my relationship to reality, I soon realized that this relationship spoke in many voices. As Barbara Newman reminds us, this is likely because the entire concept of the self was permeable in the Middle Ages. In the lectures that follow, I use the second person, *you*, as a way of showing how self-extension operates. *You* is central to the structure and syntax of the series. This *you* is sometimes the writer, sometimes the reader, and sometimes appears as an amalgamation of many. In all cases, *you* is permeable.

The other key motif that gives syntax to the series—a motif that runs like a clue, or a red herring, through each lecture—is the human hand. About a decade ago, I was introduced to a medieval teaching tool in the shape of a hand that was used to help students learn a series of new relationships. As I prepared an experimental class on medieval and digital performance—my attempt to bring the past and present into relation in a way that was shareable—I came across an arresting image of a hand covered in musical notation in an anthology entitled *The Medieval Craft of Memory* (2002). What appeared to be an image associated with some obscure esoteric tradition is an image of the Guidonian Hand (see Figure I.1). Although dubiously named after the eleventh-century Benedictine monk Guido of Arezzo (991/992– after 1033), one of the world's most famous music teachers, and the person who is attributed with the invention of the musical staff as we know it today, it is universally accepted that he is not the hand's originator. But Guido did write about its function as a mnemonic device, a pedagogical tool that helps one to remember.

In the medieval world, this hand helps a singer to remember the order of notes in a given song. It helps with sight-singing. It turns something that is heard into something that is seen. It makes the invisible world visible—a visual map of auditory space. However, the more I learned about how this hand "worked," how it was used to help singers remember the relation between notes in overlapping series of hexachords by placing these notes on the tips and joints of the fingers,

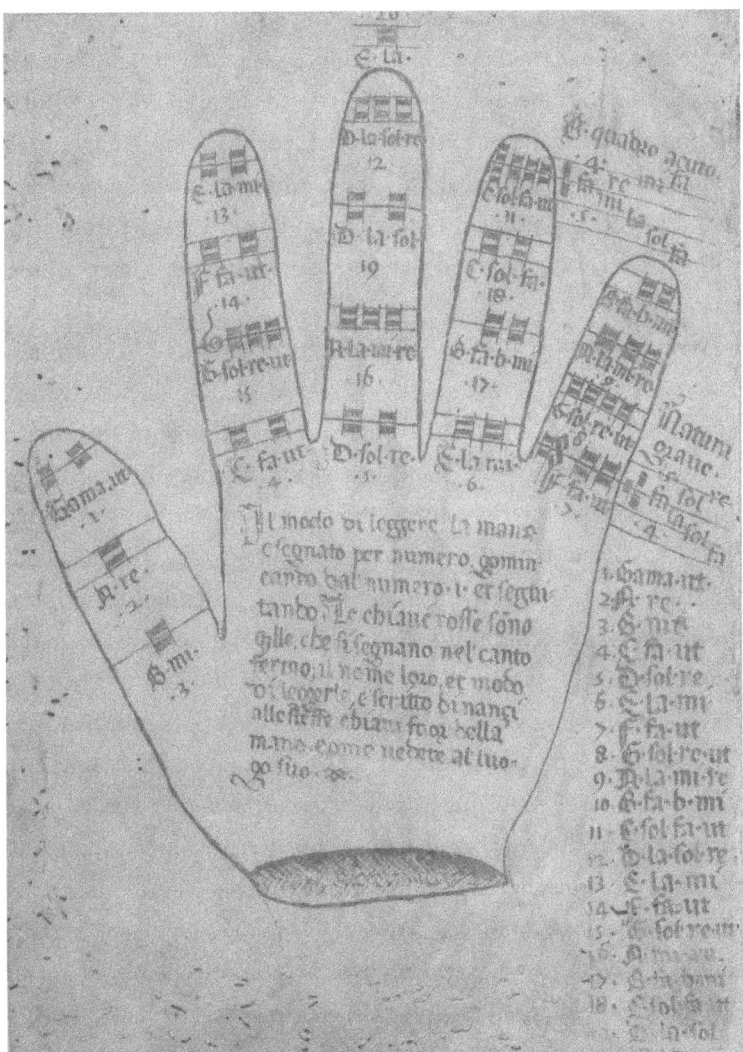

Figure I.1. Guidonian Hand with solmization syllables, *c.* sixteenth century. Courtesy of Fine Art Images/Heritage Images/Getty Images.

the less I could relate. Nevertheless, I was compelled to keep returning to this memory-hand, this aide-mémoire. How might it be helping me to remember time differently? I treated it like a Zen koan used in meditation practice to exhaust the analytic intellect and ready the mind to respond from deep intuitive knowing. It took ten years and the completion of this book before I fully understood the kind of work it was doing with me and for me. It appeared at the end of my writing process like a teacher you once believed taught you nothing, only to realize that you had internalized their teachings to such a degree that they had become your inner teacher, no longer separate from you. Ultimately, it was this hand that brought everything I learned into relation.

Writing on the Guidonian Hand in or after 1477, Johannes Tinctoris's *Expositio manus*, or "Treatise on the hand" (which sometimes reads like a treatise on synesthesia), explains this music that you can touch. The "hand is a short and useful lesson, fully showing the characteristics of sounds in music," Tinctoris explains. "The term 'hand,' however, is used as the container for the contained, for any hand, that extreme member placed at the end of the arm on the human body according to physiologists, contains that lesson in the tips and joints of its fingers" (Seay & Tinctoris 1965: 200). Tinctoris plays an interesting game of hands here. He describes the "hand" as a lesson, a medium, and as the carrier of information ("the container for the contained") implying that the external hand *and* what it carries inside itself are integral to understanding its function. In one instance, the hand is connected to a human body and his description points to its internal properties (i.e., its relationship to thought, specifically, sound thought); in another instance, it is a lesson affixed to an external representation of a hand (i.e., it is a tool). The hand, then, is a representation of an outer teacher and simultaneously points us to our inner teacher—ourselves. In essence, Tinctoris is telling us that everything we need is in our hands.

Tinctoris's treatise on the hand is, itself, part of a long philosophical tradition of writing about the hand. The hand is a human's first tool, the "tool of tools," according to Aristotle. In *De Anima*, he makes an analogy that pairs the soul with the hand: "for as the hand is the tool of tools; thought is the form of forms" (qtd in Barnes 1984: 432a, 235). Hegel thought of the hand as the "middle term" for both inner and outer (1977: 190). Next to the organ of speech, he tells us that the hand is "how man manifests and actualizes himself" (1977: 189). Francoise Meltzer tells us that "the hand is always tied to thought and to techne and therefore always engaging the dialectic of inner being and outward manifestation" (2001: 626). Rebecca Schneider theorizes that the Paleolithic hand with whom she is in relation is "performing a 'withness' that beckons both to and with the rock as well as any being who might come upon that rock as a hail" (2018: 291–2). This inclusion of the nonhuman in a discussion of the hand is an important addition to the conversation. Schneider troubles the way the hand often signifies human exceptionalism. This understanding also goes some way toward helping me to understand the kind of "withness" I experienced while thinking with and through the Guidonian Hand over the last decade. This long tradition of writing about hands that spans from Ancient Greece to the present moment holds out a marvelous list of what and how the hand allows us to think and suggests that the hand has long served as the middle term between inner and outer worlds.

Over the years that I was thinking with and through this Guidonian Hand, as my teachers showed up one by one, it put me in relationship to many other hands that are explored in this series: the hand as an instrument of the voice of god for Hildegard of Bingen (in Lecture 1); as it is depicted in the medieval paintings of the *Noli me tangere*, translated as "Do not touch" (in Lecture 2); the plaster casts made of Eleonora Duse's hands (in Lecture 3); the discussions of Simone Weil's small and clumsy hands (in Lecture 4); in Marina Abramović's first performance art piece, *Rhythm 10*, which takes place entirely on her hands (in Lecture 5); in a discussion of transgenerational trauma and Resmaa Menakem's *My Grandmother's Hands* (in Lecture 6); in Hilma af Klint's hands that channel "higher beings" from the "astral plane" who she says are responsible for her most powerful series of abstract paintings, *The Ten Largest* (in Lecture 7); and finally in a discussion of how the Guidonian Hand places the teachings of these seven lectures in relation to each other (Lecture 8).

Throughout the series, the hands, like the second person, *you*, who speaks, remembers, and listens, are entirely permeable. As they move back and forth between the lectures, new relationships are formed: the meaning of the hands is found in the questions that they generate. Hands are always relational. In the case of these lectures, they are always pointing at the mystery and never pointing in the same direction, but are always keen to make a connection. In the description of the lectures that follows, I refer to the lecturer (me) as "the writer" to signal the shifting point of view the reader will encounter in the lectures. I utilize the shifts in perspective as a way of engaging a reflexive autoethnographic approach to the research process.

***

Lecture 1, "Character Study," sets up some of the key themes that are woven throughout the eight lectures. Beginning with a discussion of character as theorized in Aristotle's *Poetics*, the writer thinks through the ways that action determines character before applying Aristotle's theory to her own "character." She goes in search of Hildegard of Bingen at a Benedictine convent on the Vermont–Québec border and reflects on some unlikely parallels between herself and Hildegard of Bingen as their "characters" are inflected through their disciplines. When their disciplines differently betray both Hildegard and the writer, she discusses how it feels to come to the end of her world while she's still living in it. Through Hildegard's own teaching and artistic example, she suggests how one's internal reality can (re)build a world from the inside-out by starting from an entirely different paradigm. In this way the first lecture ends in catastrophe and identity-death before opening into the doorway of mystery.

Lecture 2, "Genre," begins where the previous one ends—with the word *mystery*. This conceit continues throughout the series. Each lecture builds on the next, ending with a key term or idea that will then be unpacked in the subsequent lecture. Since *mystery* is the genre in which the lectures are moving, in this lecture the origins of the medieval mystery genre (i.e., the *Quem quaeritis* trope) are historicized and theorized. It is then put into conversation with medieval depictions of the *Noli me tangere*, translated "Do not touch"—a continuation of the story of Christ's rebirth recounted in the *Quem quaeritis* trope. Beginning in catastrophe, before moving through recognition and *then* reversal (see Kubiak 1991), the writer imagines the form of this mystery play genre reflecting its content: what do we do with a love that never dies? To make that love live again, the writer suggests, we dress the flesh in theatre. As the story of theatre's rebirth is reborn through the story of Christ's missing body, the writer analyzes how mixed realities—like the one Mary Magdalene experiences when she finds Jesus materialized as a gardener—allows us to posit the way theatre, like the story that gives birth to it, operates at the threshold between two worlds. *Noli me tangere* is also a story about hands—especially Christ's refusal to take Mary Magdalene's hand so that she can understand this new reality she encounters. This hand becomes a motif used to contemplate the grief of losing those whom we love, and how often in life we find ourselves in this liminal place between the known and unknown worlds. This hand, which Heidegger tells us is "meant to carry us into the great oneness," is itself carried over to the next lecture on *gesture*.

In Lecture 3, "Gesture," the writer begins with a discussion of Stanislavski's *An Actor Prepares* (1936) to unpack the challenges that face young acting students when asked about the difficulties of their craft—the question of what to do with their hands is a perennial problem. The treatment of hands and actor training segues into an introduction of Eleonora Duse—the first modern actor in the Western world and the source of what is now largely understood as the basis of Stanislavsky's system of actor training. Newspaper clippings found in Duse's archive at the University of Glasgow recount in iterative detail the wonders of her beautiful hands. The writer then gets obsessed with a photograph of a plaster cast made of Duse's hand—a cast that resembles a medieval relic in the age of mechanical reproduction. Just as Mary Magdalene tries to grasp Jesus's hand to follow him into the afterlife, Duse's plaster hand sends the writer to an Afterlife Awareness Conference in Orlando, Florida. Linking the writer's own introduction to—and fascination with—end-of-life doulas and afterlife awareness to Duse's experiences of dying over and over on the stage, the writer charts her own experiences through Duse's movements.

The final third of the lecture is given to an examination of Duse's interest in film, which she studies ardently after quitting the theatre at the age of fifty. In exploring her only film, *Cenere* (1916), the writer sees in Duse a similar preoccupation with the dramatization of Christ's death—how in middle age Duse also becomes a bit obsessed with the Middle Ages. In fact, Duse wishes to place her own body in the place of Jesus as he is depicted in medieval images of his crucifixion. Yet, she is frustrated with the medium of film that she finds so alienating. As she writes in a letter to her friend Giorgio Papini, "life is not cinema" (qtd in Vacche 2008: 138). Despite her alienation from this medium, it is through *Cenere* that Duse's gestures, her hands, and her immersion into medieval images is ultimately kept alive in another way: film suggests another kind of afterlife.

Frustrated by the contradictions in the life and writing of Simone Weil, in Lecture 4, "Alienation," the writer turns to Brecht's alienation effect to contemplate her alienation from this figure before becoming preoccupied with Weil's death, and then training as an end-of-life doula. As this lecture is now close to the middle of the series, the writer begins with a question that is often used to analyze a play text: What changes? What moment or image must the writer pass through to get from the beginning to the end of her story? Ultimately, this lecture is about the writer's attempt to come to some sort of recognition—to recognize herself in Weil or have Weil offer some clue as to how they are in relationship. While the writer keeps looking for some personal connection, it is when she takes seriously Weil's own philosophy alongside the concept of Brecht's alienation effect that another kind of recognition takes place that allows the writer to move forward. The writer ends by placing herself in an imagined dialogue with Weil's favorite Greek philosopher, Pythagoras, to discuss the number five and the work of the hands. In doing so, she enacts the theme of the next lecture: acting and not acting.

The writer commences Lecture 5, "On Acting and Not Acting," with a discussion of the historical context of the medieval mystery play performances, using the York cycle as example. This allows her to unpack some of the relationships between Brecht's alienation effect and the duality present in medieval acting theory (see Aronson-Lehavi 2011). She then jumps from discussing behavior on the stage to behaviors in everyday life—especially those that we unconsciously inherit. Reflecting on the suicide of a performance artist friend who was also a proponent of using religious ritual in his work, the writer thinks about the relationship between acting and the *real* work of the performance artist. She wonders if an understanding of medieval acting theory may have been useful to her friend before admitting her failure to understand his decision.

Turning to Marina Abramović's work (and her obsession with her own death), the writer attempts to find a critical distance to understand her friend, but instead finds that Abramović is a kind of placeholder for her own family inheritance. Linking the methods of Family Constellation therapy (that works with transgenerational trauma) to Abramović's own life and work, the writer analyzes Abramović's first performance art piece, *Rhythm 10* (1973). The piece, which takes place entirely on her hands, performs a kind of traumatic and violent repetition that is witnessed by the audience in performance. In the witnessing, Abramović discovers an aspect of herself that she had not previously met—an aspect that is inseparable from her relationship to the audience. In bearing witness in some oblique way to her own familial history of transgenerational trauma, the interdependence between Abramović and the spectators brings something new into consciousness. The writer ends by considering how often we are other to ourselves, always already double, and how this confrontation forces us to reflect on the ways that *we* are the mystery we seek.

In Lecture 6, "The Theatre and Its Double," the writer places discussions of transgenerational trauma alongside her ancestors' participation in the slave trade. Beginning with a discussion of Resmaa Menekem's *My Grandmother's Hands: Racialized Trauma and the Pathways to Mending Our Hearts and Bodies* (2017), she reflects on how the medieval trauma of her ancestors in Europe (discussed in Menekam) might have been transferred and enacted on nonwhite bodies in the American colonies. Using the figure of Frederick Douglass escaping slavery in 1845 on a ship called *The Cambria* that begins her previous work, *Kinship and Performance in the Black and Green Atlantic* (2014), the writer explores a soldier who came to Douglass's aid: Capt. Thomas Gough. Gough shares a surname with her slaveholding ancestors. This kicks off a discussion of doubles and how we must confront our own darkness as part of both a personal and a collective inheritance. Digging deeper into her own childhood experiences of fractured race relations and what she knows of her family's history, the writer looks to Artaud's *The Theatre and Its Double* (1958) to consider gnostic estrangement—how the "realism" we endure in the theatre works at a distance from the reality that is experienced in the world.

This challenge between how reality is portrayed and the doubles it obscures is not only manifest in the relationship between her ancestors and Capt. Thomas Gough, but also in another Thomas whose 'reality' obscures a double. The writer places the figure of the Doubting Thomas in conversation with the gnostic Gospel of Thomas (discovered in Nag Hammadi in 1945) that announces that *this* Thomas is the "double" and the "twin." Unlike the Thomas who does not believe that Christ returned from the dead, this gnostic scribe announces to his readers that those who grasp the meaning of this text "will not know the taste of death." The writer ends by contemplating Caravaggio's hyperrealistic *Incredulity of Thomas* (1601–2), an image that is also about the work of the hands. It is a baroque theatrical image that forces us to question the ways that Caravaggio uses the hands in the painting to play with death. Caravaggio's Thomas, who is incredulous and full of doubt, shares intimations with the gnostic Thomas (a theatrical double) who is the secret scribe of a nondualistic lineage that shares Jesus's secret teachings. Given Caravaggio's interest in using his contemporaries as models for biblical figures in his work, there is the suggestion here that we, too, hovering between doubt and a mystery, play and death, are Thomas.

Lecture 7, "*Duende*, or Play and Death," begins in a dream featuring a dead painter whose current retrospective is taking place at the Guggenheim. The writer attempts to understand Hilma af Klint, attends a course on the foundations of mediumship in the outskirts of London, and then heads to New York to see *Hilma af Klint: Paintings for the Future* (2018–19). Researching af Klint's life and work, the writer finds surprising parallels between the change in af Klint's artistic process in middle age and her own change in direction. Af Klint's interest in mediumship and her channeling of "astral beings" who, according to af Klint, guide her hands in a series of paintings entitled *The Ten Largest* (1907), force the writer to consider af Klint's artistic intentions—her process of letting go of her training, or letting go of expectations and outcomes. With paintbrush in hand, she remains curious about the unseen life she might be painting into existence. The writer continues to chart the way that af Klint is teaching her a similar trick, a way of unmaking her own artistic discipline and unmaking herself in the process. For af Klint, the practices she embarks upon in the second half of her life are simultaneously the content of her further research: her artistic practice and her creations are the way that she lives her mystery. In charting this process, the writer, echoing the first lecture on Hildegard, is given another paradigm for how our disciplines and processes can unmake us. This time, with a sense that the only way to stay present to our own death is to play.

In the final lecture, "*Theatron*: The Seeing Place," the writer traces her journey through the previous lectures by situating herself in the dramaturgical framework of The Last Judgment, the play that typically ends a mystery play cycle. In coming to terms with the end of her world—a world where she imagined herself as a protagonist only to find that it was simply a play-world that is now being deconstructed by stagehands—she sees that it is finally time to play her last hand. The Guidonian Hand appears here as a way of reminding the writer and the reader that they have completed the whole gamut. That is, the Hand is used to teach students how to remember a series of seven overlapping hexachords. Here it is reimagined by the writer to remember the teachings of the seven overlapping lectures in her series.

Notes

1 Medieval mystery plays are biblical plays that are typically performed in a cycle. In York, where the records are the most robust, there are forty-eight surviving plays from Genesis to the Last Judgment. The nomenclature of the "mystery plays" is two-fold: "mysteries" are understood as holding hidden, mystical significance, and "mystery" was also the name used interchangeably with the trade guilds who sponsored and performed the plays.
2 It is interesting to note that this trope—sung phrases and sentences added to various parts of the liturgy as embellishment—appears

simultaneously in various locations throughout Europe, and over the tenth century, manifests as the *Visitatio Sepulchri*, or the *Quem quaeritis* trope. While the *Visitatio Sepulchri* is based on the bible, the story follows neither Matthew, Mark, Luke nor John. James Forse (2002: 59) tells us that the "harmonizing" of gospel stories in this way would have served to condense and dramatize to congregations the essential message of the event. In other words, in the *Visitatio Sepulchri* story, this "harmonized" history *only* exists as (music) theatre.

3 "The Norse knew Meashowe by a different name. Shortly after Christmas 1153, Earl Harald Maddadarson was travelling over land from Hamnavoe (Stromness) to Firth (the Finstown area). Caught in a snowstorm, he and his men took shelter in 'Orkahaugr,' and the location of Maeshowe fits the story as described in the *Orkneyinga Saga*" written about 50 years later, in the early 1200s (Pickering & Foster 2022: 18). A sample of translated carvings are "The man who is most skilled in runes west of the ocean carved these runes with the axe which Gauk Trandilson owned in the south of the country [Iceland]," "Ofram Sigurdsson carved these runes," and "Benedikt made this cross" (Pickering & Foster 2022: 19).

4 In the fall 2020 semester, my curiosity about the relationship between education and healing hit its edge when teaching continued online and faculty, staff, and students were showing signs of extreme suffering. I briefly hosted a series of Zoom conversations entitled "Being Liminal" aimed at giving my students different frameworks for understanding their lived reality at that moment. The second conversation, "Education and the Art of Healing," which aired in October 2020, was comprised of a performance studies scholar and therapist, a performance philosopher and grief worker, an education professor, a psychology professor, and a psychiatrist. You can find a recording of that conversation here: <https://www.youtube.com/watch?v=K70ldx7zX-4> accessed June 20, 2023.

Lecture 1

Character Study

Remember the time we are in class, and you discuss Aristotle's *Poetics*, particularly the way he talks about character? You can have a tragedy without character, he says (though you're paraphrasing from a translation), but (and this is important, you say) you can't have a tragedy without action. Aristotle firmly believes that character comes in as a subsidiary to action. Later, you can't stop thinking about this, especially since you are preparing character studies.

If you take this whole idea outside of the world of the play, and consider it as life, for instance, like, maybe the life you are leading when you are on that sabbatical that takes you to the brink of, well, what exactly? It's still hard to know. You tell me that during this time there is nothing stable about your identity. You keep appearing in places that are "uncharacteristic" (your word), and that's what keeps it interesting (for you, but maybe for me, too), the fact that the activities are not in keeping with your character. This time you define that as "disposition," or "temperament."

Just like in a play, many times in life, we understand our own drama through actions and obstacles: what does a character want, and what is in the way? Performances are always relational, there is always a desire, and always an obstacle to that desire, even if the performer is solo, even if she is not acknowledging the audience, everything is still relational. All the same, I prefer it if you and I are acknowledged.

You tell me that this is why you keep comparing yourself to that artist. Unlike that artist who is a painter, theatre is the medium that takes you into the mystery. You know, the language of theatre—how the story is plotted, the way we must suspend disbelief, the way nothing in a story happens by accident (even accident).

So what if you mapped out your journey via dramatic action, noting the obstacles, the accidents?

Still too big, you say. Start small, you say.

Character study. How one comes to understand a character. What if the character you don't understand is yourself? What if the character seems like it's going in five directions at once? Is it an incoherent character? A weak character? Or is it a foil? Like a character that's pulled into a story to help you understand the protagonist, who is, it is always implied, the *real* character?

Several years ago, while you are in therapy, you tell me you are surprised to discover that you are writing in your journal in the second person. To this day you still don't know if you are writing to M— (the therapist), or yourself. Either way, you wonder about this other person who's with you.

You say it is maybe not so much a person, but something like a second *persona* narrator. *Persona* comes from the Ancient Greek word that means "mask," literally *a thing to sound through*, you say, avoiding my hard eye roll.

This second person surprises you. You tell me you don't even notice at first. But then, one day, you look back through months of your journal and see that it has been your story for quite a while.

Does this mean you are also a character, you wonder? Or, maybe you're just acting *as if* you are a character, since, of course, you are not, or, not according to Aristotle, who, while not denying the importance of character, still lets us know that we can go through a whole drama without one.

But not really. Characters are still vehicles for action, and you can't figure out someone's character if they're just sitting there. You need to *do* something! And in all honesty, you're just sitting here reading this sentence I wrote ages ago. But you can still suspend disbelief.

You, along with the character who is sometimes also called *you*, can, through this suspension, inhabit the same reality. This still requires action. Aristotle was right about that. At least, there's no way for you to meet these characters without a desire to enter their reality, and without stumbling upon a number of obstacles. Or maybe you are trying to stumble into my reality, and are also hitting some obstacles? This begs the question: who's the actual protagonist of this story? From whose point of view are you to understand the action? One point of view feels so limited, don't you think?

This drama may work without characters, but we do need *personas*. Sure, they're just a bunch of masks, but *personas* do make some sounds and that's something, you suppose.

***

You wonder if there is something specific to tragedy that requires action to come before character? Like, do you ever look back on a tragic event in your life and think, that changed me, I'm not the same person I was before that happened? The event does not need to be an Oedipus-sized tragedy, you know, with a plague, and citizens dying, and no one taking care of it, and the leader thinking it's everyone but him (spoiler alert: it's him). Maybe the "event" is not even one thing because at the time you don't actually know there is a tragedy coming, you're just performing a series of actions that lead to your downfall without you knowing it.

You're speaking as if we are in a play, and you see that it's confusing me because a play is not real life.

You tell me a story about a former teacher—geography professor—who often kicks off the discussion of the week's reading by asking the class, "What is the dream of the writer?" If you pause for too long, she might add, "Where's the love y'all?" No one ever asks you this before, even though intuitively you know that if something is worth writing, there is a dream attached, and if something is worth reading, it is to your benefit to understand that dream, to enter it with the writer and explore the world. What you learn from her question is that the dreamworlds we enter need not be fictional. They can just as easily take place in the world, in actual geographical space. They can ask you to imagine reality from a paradigm so different from your common sense that the mere existence of such a place often feels like a liberation, reminding you of how little you know about who you are and what you're doing here…

You trail off.

You come back.

All of this is to say that theatre is a world-building project, and when you follow certain characters you can't forget the conventions of their world, the world they bring into being right here on earth.

You tell me that at the beginning of your sabbatical you stay at a cloistered Benedictine Monastery because you are searching for a medieval mystic, Hildegard of Bingen (1098–1179).

You should know that time and space work differently on this planet.

You mean your sabbatical-planet? Who's the character here?

You read so much about her, but it doesn't get you anywhere. Every book provides facts about her character, you suppose, but not really anything about the actions that create her character.[1] It's a hunch, but you think that visiting a convent where nuns still say their prayers eight times a day by singing Gregorian chant (can you sing a chant? or do you chant a song?) might help you to explore her music and visions.[2] Do the actions of chanting or singing take her to other worlds where she then produces all those compositions? The compositions that make her the first-known musical composer in the Western world?[3] You do some research to see if a convent like this still exists. Would you believe it—there is a cloistered nunnery that still practices this tradition a ninety-minute drive away?

You arrive at the convent, and as you walk through the door, a voice tells you that there is nothing inevitable about you being here. Second thing to note: *people hear voices on this planet.*

You remember another time you had this experience with the voices, four years earlier. You arrive at a ten-day silent meditation retreat—a retreat you never think you have the desire or capacity to attend. Walking toward the building, you hear a voice say, "I can't believe you made it!" Is it your voice? It's an excited voice, a voice that does not think that your being there will be a possibility. The voice does not say: "this is not supposed to happen," or "I always know you will make it here," but expresses a level of incredulity: "I can't believe you made it!" You like to think that the voice is announcing that now, now that you *have* made it, anything is possible.

Whether it's a grueling ten-day Buddhist meditation retreat or attending prayers eight times a day to follow the Gregorian chanting of the nuns, one thing you realize is that this world is hard work. Sure, voices emerge from thin air, there's the feeling of mystery all around you, but it takes discipline. You're not sure you have it. Actually, you're mostly certain that you don't.

***

Does discipline build character? Is it through discipline that we understand character? You must admit, discipline is a tricky word. You can say that Hildegard's discipline takes her somewhere else, but this, too, is two-fold. You wonder if her discipline is her activity of prayer and chanting or if her discipline is music, as a field of study or expertise. For that matter, her discipline could be medicine, or biblical exegesis, or dramatic composition. In many respects, she is lucky to live in a world where there are few borders between disciplines, even if they are all punishing and there is no penicillin.

Is a "field of study" as a "discipline" the same as the "activity or exercise of discipline"? You think there is some distinction here, but you've been institutionalized for so long—*no, you say, not there, you idiot, in the academy*, that you no longer know.

You're defensive about my joke.

What intrigues you about this question, and the world in which this question is important, is that depending on what you emphasize it can lead you in different directions. And these two directions point to whether Aristotle is correct that character comes in as a subsidiary to action, or whether we can understand someone's actions by first knowing their character. Are we simply the product of our actions?

You seem to be speaking to yourself now, or the place in front of you and just above your head. Either way, it always comes back to Aristotle.

The first definition the *Oxford English Dictionary* gives for "discipline" is found in a copy of the Rule of St. Benedict from 1225, the rule that Hildegard follows from the time she is tithed to the Benedictine monastery at the age of eight. She is the tenth child, the story goes, so her parents give ten percent of what they own to the church: they give Hildegard as an oblate. The first definition says, "sense related to punishment, or instrument of punishment; a whip, scourge." Not an auspicious start. The next definition reads, "senses relating to training, instruction, or method." And then you see what you are looking for, which is more fitting with your character: "Instruction as given to disciples, scholars; schooling, teaching. Also: the result of this; education, learning." Curious that the first two mention the "senses" while the third, the one that you've been "tithed" to since the age of eighteen, begins with "instruction." Does instruction not require the senses? You begin to see the problem with your discipline.

Hildegard is an anchoress from the age of eight, walled up inside a living tomb with women committed to the renunciation of worldly things. Here, she learns to read and write and pray. She takes vows as a Benedictine nun at age eighteen and is unanimously voted the new magistra in 1136, after her beloved teacher, Jutta, dies. At this point, she's about thirty-eight years old, which is four or five years before it all gets cosmic. There's no better narrator of Hildegard's medieval midlife crisis than Hildegard herself (translated from the Latin, you say). You really get how time and space work on her planet here:

> And behold! In the forty-third year of my earthly course, as I was gazing with great fear and trembling attention at a heavenly vision, I saw a great splendor in which resounded a voice from Heaven, saying to me,
>
> "O fragile human, ashes of ashes, filth of filth! Say and write what you see and hear. ...] Explain these things in such a way that the hearer, receiving the words of his instructor, may expound them in those words, according to that will, vision and instruction. ...
>
> It happened that, in the eleven hundred and forty-first year of the Incarnation of the Son of God, Jesus Christ, when I was forty-two and seven months old, Heaven was opened and the fiery light of exceeding brilliance came and permeated my whole brain, and inflamed my whole heart and my whole breast, not like a burning but like a warming flame, as the sun warms anything its rays touch. And immediately I knew the meaning of the exposition of the Scriptures ...
>
> But I, though I saw and heard these things, refused to write for a long time through doubt and bad opinion and the diversity of human words, not with stubbornness but in the exercise of humility, until, laid low by the scourge of God, I fell upon a bed of sickness; then, compelled at last by many illnesses, ... I set my hand to writing. While I was doing it, I sensed, as I mentioned before, the deep profundity of scriptural exposition; and, raising myself from illness by the strength I received, I brought this work to a close—though just barely—in ten years. (1990: 59–61; see Figure 1.1)

It is a big ask of one person. Hildegard has zero desire to write. The voice demands it of her. She can very well ignore the voice, you suspect, would ignore it until her death, you emphasize, if it wasn't for those terrible headaches. There's a fine line between mysticism and madness and she knows it. Many will think she's mad. She knows she hasn't a choice. She can't live with those migraines and that voice.

Figure 1.1. Illumination from Hildegard's *Scivias* depicting her receiving a vision and dictating the message to Volmar, her male secretary, 1151.

You're sounding less like a scholar than a confidant. Are we in a play here?

She's about forty-three years old when this goes down, you say, ignoring my question. You mention that you're slightly younger than forty-three when you find her. You stay interested in her, are compelled by her, because of this change in direction in her forties, this need to write, and not just write (because she wrote many letters and other things aside before the age of forty-three), but write down her visions, to bring her dreamworld to earth, because she can't ignore the pain or the voice or her own true nature.[4]

You wonder if Hildegard ever thinks her discipline betrays her.

What is it to lose your discipline? Have you ever felt betrayed by your discipline? These are some questions that come up for you when you think of Hildegard's disciplined monastic world. What you mean is that she follows the Rule of St. Benedict—the self-punishment, the study, the listening, the prayer, the chanting—with exactitude. Then sometime in middle age her discipline turns on her, or turns her inside out, or turns the discipline inside out, which may all be the same thing at this point.

Her world has structure, there is form, it is about repetition, it keeps her safe, she knows and practices the rules. She becomes the *abbess* for fuck's sake. She *is* the rules! Hildegard knows how time and space work on this planet, how they are kept in place through the practice of the disciplines. But in her forties, she sees her time is up. All of her discipline takes her somewhere terrifying, and mind-stopping, and electrifying, and maybe lonely, too, because no one else in her world sees and hears how and what she sees and hears. They're still safe in their discipline.

She stays in bed for so long because she knows it is the end of her world, and you can't stop thinking maybe that's why you do, too.

You hand me notes for a lecture you write and never deliver. You tell me to read it and that I'll understand why.

***

The Annunciation of Hildegard of Bingen

I am walking through the door of the Monastery of the Immaculate Heart of Mary[5] when I hear a voice whisper in my ear, "there's nothing inevitable about you being here." Then a nun greets me cheerily and shows me to my room for the next four days.

In this cloistered Benedictine convent on the Vermont–Québec border, the good sisters structure their day according to the sonic rhythms familiar to my twelfth-century Benedictine heroine, Hildegard of Bingen (1098–1179).

Among other things, Hildegard writes seventy liturgical songs and our first known morality play. She becomes a doctor of the church on October 12, 2012, seven years after I become a doctor of performance studies. Nine hundred years earlier, Hildegard is an anchoress, walled inside a living tomb. In Hildegard's day, it is customary for a bishop to say the Office of the Dead when an anchoress takes her vows—a symbolic death to worldly things.

She learns to read and write and pray. A sympathetic monk passes her books on botany and medicine through the cell's small window. It is one of the gendered secrets of medieval monastic life that this living tomb gives her access to more knowledge than most women in the whole of Europe.

In 1136, she is named *magistra*, or spiritual teacher, and gets a promotion: no longer anchoress, but abbess. A little later, she also hears from God. *Again*. This time he tells her that she needs to start writing down everything she hears and sees. She does not want to do this. She finally says "yes" when she, like me, is in her forties. Her suffering is too great to bear saying "no" any longer. Afterward, she is one of the most prolific creative forces the world has ever known.

So begins the Annunciation of Hildegard of Bingen.

I sit in a chapel by myself. I forget that the nuns are cloistered, that we will not share a chapel. Ahead and to my left I see their shadows move behind an iron gate.

I am here to follow the Latin prayers that punctuate the day at eight intervals, sung in Gregorian chant. The list in my room reads as follows:

Vigils
Lauds
Prime
Holy Mass
Sext
None
Vespers
Compline

Listening to the chanting, I think of the first annunciation, the one Hildegard sets to song. The plot is simple: Gabriel arrives from his dimension and appears before a young woman to announce some game-changing news. Mary's job, should she choose to accept it, is to give birth to a whole new consciousness. She's a teenager. She must be terrified. Still, she says *yes, I will, Yes.*

As I listen to the Gregorian chanting through the bars of the iron gate, I don't feel I have a face.

The *Rule of Saint Benedict* begins, "Listen carefully to the master's instructions, and attend to them with the ear of your heart" (Benedict 1931). I hear this phrase for the first time while practicing with a group of silent Sufis in Northern California. Sufis know how to listen like this. It is no easy matter.

I return from chapel, and in the silence of my room I re-read Henry Corbin's "Mundus Imaginalis" (1975). Philosopher, theologian, and late professor of Islamic Studies, Corbin is also interested in a twelfth-century mystic, a Sufi by the name of Suhrawardī. Corbin coins the phrase "*mundus imaginalis*," to indicate a precise order of reality that corresponds to a precise mode of perception. "Between the empirical world and the world of abstract understanding there is," according to Corbin, "an intermediate world." This world is as real as the world of the senses and the world of the intellect.

Iranian Sufis refer to this world as "the eighth climate," or "No-where." I have an acute sense that Hildegard reaches the eighth climate during the eight periods of chanting each day. That she rides the wave of sound into some kind of *directionless time-field* (Stockhausen 1959: 36) where she sees her visions with her ears.

Corbin's essay is the most difficult I ever assign to undergraduates. One student finally asks the question I know is on the tongue of the room: "Do you actually believe they travel to this place?" The question, in part, a check of my academic credentials. My impartiality. But I also hear something that sounds like longing. So, I tell him that belief in the imaginal world is dependent on how seriously we take our internal reality.

"What is an internal reality?" The class looks up, curious. I bring in Tibetan singing bowls. We practice seeing with our ears, we practice staying in liminal space: sitting, listening, not knowing. Everything happens in this space. Nothing happens in this space. Do we have enough time? How much longer can we avoid the *tyranny of the quantifiable*? (Solnit 2014: 97)[6]

In the twelfth century, Hildegard is alive to see the birth of the university system, which, for women, is the death of higher education for the better part of the next millennium. I listen to the birth of the university from astride the grave. Women eclipsed from the small shaft of light that is available to some in that century. I begin my university education in the last decade of a millennium that begins with Hildegard's birth. Hildegard and I are among the first generation of women in the history of the world to hold a doctorate in the same number as men. A 900-year experiment arising, passing away, arising, passing away.

There is nothing inevitable about me being here. But I am here.

I make a quick note to myself when I return from the monastery. I find it in my journal while writing these notes almost two years later:

> Monday, September 24, 2018: The university has been a kind of monastery for me—an institution that takes care as long as you follow its exacting rules and move your life wherever it may take you. It has served me well. I am one of the lucky few women who can say this. Being at the monastery and attending mass I feel like I am peering back on the life of an intimate stranger; it's over 30 years since my regular attendance in this ritual. In the future, I feel university life will appear like this to me.

***

You tell me that this is why you can't answer the question about who the character is in this story, or whose play you're in right now. You think you're searching for Hildegard, but after you arrive, you're lost. You hear voices, then you lose your face. Afterward, you know nothing. You lose your discipline at that monastery. Your rigorous, methodical, disciplined way of conducting research leads to your indiscipline, or antidiscipline, or unconscious uncoupling from your discipline. It's dangerous in a way, this being taken somewhere else, the way some disciplines break something open not through study, but through action.

Then not long after that visit you find yourself in a yurt in rural Vermont taking a sound healing course. *Sound healing.*[7] Tibetan singing bowls vibrating on your body. The bowls are beautiful—they're incredible—but you are *not. this. character.* Except that apparently, you are.

Aristotle 1 – You 0

After the first day you can't sleep—at midnight, 1 AM, 2 AM, you still hear the bowls, still *feel* them in your body. You wonder sometimes if they ever stopped, or if you have grown accustomed to the sound…

You digress.

The curious thing about being at the end of your world while you are still living in it, is that there is no escape. Hildegard doesn't take off. Nothing exists outside of her world. There is no prison break, no side hustle for a Benedictine abbess. Everything changes but she's in the same life, or, at least, that's how it appears. But that's just appearance.

Her internal reality redesigns the outer reality. That's the incredible truth of her world, that there is no such thing as inside and outside. Like a Möbius strip, each turns into the other.

I mean, she *is* dead but that's no match for her character. She dies when her world ends, and yet, there she is, with her character still kicking. Can't be afraid when you're already dead. The Sufis call this ego death *dying before you die*. Come to think of it, surely other people call it this too.

When her world ends, she shape-shifts into a bridge. She manages to make her internal reality the new norm. Not just *her* new norm, but *everybody's* new norm.

You start to get really excited about this, maybe too excited.

The voices that only she hears, the music that plays only for her, the exquisite images that blind her with their light—she takes everyone along for the ride. Here's the paradox, though you're unsure if it is a real paradox. This isn't a magic carpet ride: she takes everyone along for the ride by redirecting their discipline. She makes her *inner* world into their *outer* reality through *their* actions: Volmar, her male secretary, writes down the visions that she dictates; the nuns who are skilled in painting create the gorgeous images that she supervises; the nuns sing the music she composes; and all of them, including Volmar, the only man, perform in the first-known morality play, her *Ordo Virtutum*, of *The Order of the Virtues*.

Whether it is drama, or music, or painting, or visionary-theological writing, these are all templates, teaching tools, that allow others to join her by making these arts into disciplines; exercises, that, when practiced repeatedly, and with rigor, take her acolytes to another world, a world that they are now co-creating with her. This world is still hard work, but each artistic discipline is now like a piece of a cosmic cartographer's map. A world-building enterprise that now makes life less boring, full of more color, and light, and music, and, crucially, you say, *mystery*.

Notes

1 While my methodology required a firsthand account of Benedictine monastic life, there are several biographies and critical works that illuminate various elements of Hildegard of Bingen's life and accomplishments with depth and texture. See Caroline Walker Bynum (1990), Fiona Maddock (2001), and Barbara Newman (1985, 1990).
2 Musical thinking is so much a part of Benedictine monastic life that even the religious services are divided into what is called the "Law of Octaves."
3 Hildegard of Bingen remained a relatively obscure religious figure until she was "rediscovered" in the 1990s through her music (especially *Symphonia*) and her one music-drama (*Ordo Virtutum*), a morality play written over a century before that genre was known, and the first medieval drama with a named author for both music and text. In 1996, Meredith Monk released an album called *Monk and the Abbess*—a beyond-the-grave collaboration with the twelfth-century mystic, and in 1998 no fewer than three productions of Hildegard's *Ordo Virtutum* appeared in New York in a variety of styles (including a "downtown" version by a group who called themselves the "Hildegurls"). A quick search on Apple Music lists upward of thirty albums from various artists covering Hildegard's vast musical corpus.
4 After the age of forty-three, Hildegard of Bingen became a prolific and creative force: she is hailed as a scientist, a healer, a prophet, a mystic, a dramatist, a musician, and a writer of a staggering genre of work. While she is best known for her seventy liturgical songs and three massive volumes that record her visions, she also wrote an encyclopedia of

medicine and natural science, two saints' lives, several occasional works, a body of hundreds of letters to people at all levels of society, and the first known morality play.

5   The Monastery of the Immaculate Heart of Mary is a cloistered Benedictine convent located in Westfield, Vermont. It is part of the Solesmes Congregation and traces its origins to St. Cecilia's Abbey, and the eleventh-century Abbaye Saint-Pierre de Solemes, both in France.

6   This is a phrase coined by Chip Ward and quoted by Rebecca Solnit (2014) in *Men Explain Things to Me*. The extract is: "The tyranny of the quantifiable is partly the failure of language and discourse to describe more complex, subtle, and fluid phenomena, as well as the failure of those who shape opinions and make decisions to understand and value these slipperier things. It is difficult, sometimes even impossible, to value what cannot be named or described, and so the task of naming and describing is an essential one in any revolt against the status quo of capitalism and consumerism" (2014: 97).

7   The resonance between Gregorian chant as a form of sound healing on par with Tibetan singing bowls was made clear to me while reading Jonathan Goldman's *Healing Sounds: The Power of Harmonics* (1992). In a chapter entitled, "Harmonics and Meditation: Listening as Transformation," he recounts the story of a Benedictine monastery in France. The story goes that after the second Vatican Council in the early 1960s, the new abbot at the monastery "thought that the six to eight hours of chanting which the monks engaged in served no useful purpose and the chanting ceased" (1992: 75). Within a short space of time, the monks became alarmingly depressed and fatigued; they were also losing their hearing. Many had difficulty continuing with their work, which, for this community, took place over a twenty-hour day. Despite the long hours, over the last several centuries the work had not been a problem. After several attempts to discover the cause of the problem, a physician by the name of Dr. Alfred Tomatis was called to the community to see if he could help. When he learned that they had ceased their chanting practice, he helped to re-establish it. Soon afterward, "the monks were able to resume their twenty-hour workdays" (1992: 76), and their hearing improved. According to Dr. Tomatis, one of the main functions of the ear is to charge the brain. There are sounds that drain energy and

fatigue the listener, and there are others sounds that "charge" the listener. Sounds "which contain high frequency harmonics, such as those found in Gregorian chants, are extremely beneficial." According to Tomatis's research, it is the high frequencies found at around 8,000 Hz that "are capable of charging the central nervous system and the cortex of the brain" (1992: 75). Gregorian chant contains all the frequencies of the voice spectrum—from 70 Hz up to 9,000 Hz.

Lecture 2

Genre

Mystery is an interesting genre and is a bit like discipline. Depending on what definition you use, you can be taken in different directions. Discipline is so rich because in one direction it leads to freedom, and in another to containment, though you're not sure this is entirely true for everyone, perhaps just for you.

For a long time now, you've had a theory that almost everything in life functions like a play. If you know what genre you are inhabiting when acting out different moments in your life, you can figure out a lot about what is going on around you. Consider how, when an event occurs, you might say something like: "This is melodramatic," or "This is surreal," or "This is farcical," or "This is *tragic!*" Investigate that. It might be that you have stumbled into a story that has particular conventions that you cannot escape if you stay in that genre because that is how the genre works. Those are the rules of engagement.

This brings you to that all-important question: "what is a mystery?" You think you know, and yet, mystery is often not as it appears. If you consult the *Oxford English Dictionary*, you find that in the thirteenth century, the term "mystery" means something with hidden or mystical significance, or a religious truth known only by divine revelation.

Not exactly what you expect, is it? You suspect Hildegard of Bingen knows this mystery. You say that when you stumble into Hildegard's world at the convent, you wonder if you accidentally enter this brand of mystery yourself.

Of course, your attraction to mystery precedes your trip to find Hildegard of Bingen. Your favorite subject to teach is the rebirth of theatre in the Middle Ages, the reemergence of theatre in the West through the Christian Mass, which is all about the mystery play.

Students are often delighted to see the phrase "medieval mystery plays" on the syllabus and eagerly volunteer to present on said plays thinking, more often than not, that they will be reading a medieval version of a Scooby Doo episode, or, perhaps, even a Swedish crime novel. In any case, the expectation is that the drama will take you on a journey where there is a mystery that will be solved by the end of the play.

You tell me that this is a reasonable assumption, and one that in life frustrates you, this inability to find resolution.

This mystery is to be lived and not to be solved, you tell your students. But your discipline requires results. Can you tell your students to live the questions and then ask for answers on the midterm?

You're not sure.

You tell me that the challenge—perhaps the insurmountable obstacle to your desires—is that what your character wants, and what is in the way is also determined by genre.

"Results" are not a goal, nay-, not even thinkable in this mystery play paradigm, which means your external world is not thinkable in the genre in which you are now living, or, at least, intuit that you are now living, which, of course, cannot be confirmed, because it is (you look tired), a *mystery*.

***

One of the most mysterious things about the mystery plays, and curiously a thing that is rarely discussed, is that in this genre, people can rise from the dead.

No, not like that, wrong genre. They rise from the dead like theatre rises from the dead. It still seems, well, mysterious, that theatre reemerges, is reborn even, in the Christian Mass in AD 900, and that it does so to tell a story of a dematerialized body who is alive in another way.

What is it to be alive in another way? How can you be sure you're alive differently? And where exactly are you?

You tell me that there is a well-established story in the annals of theatre history regarding the reemergence of drama in the West following those pesky "Dark Ages." The story goes that sometime in the early tenth century, following in the wake of the great Emperor Charlemagne (who united most of Western Europe for the first time since the Fall of Rome), the Christian Church wished to play a part in what was considered the revival of civilization. One of the ways that this manifested in the Christian Mass was the practice of adding unauthorized sung phrases and sentences to various parts of the liturgy as embellishment. While these "tropes," as they were called, were never officially recognized and were local in origin, they soon appeared regularly in masses throughout Christian Europe.

One of the most important tropes, the *Quem quaeritis* (translated as "Whom do you seek?") is now considered the seedling-drama from which grew vernacular drama in the West. Also known by the title *Visitatio Sepulchri* (a visit to the tomb), this trope was originally sung in call-and-response half choirs, probably situated on either side of the central approach to the altar; the altar functioned as the space of Christ's tomb. The trope is a sung dramatization by two or three Marys (who, by the end of the tenth century, would be played by two or three Mary-monks) who visit the tomb of Christ only to be told by one or two angels (played by one or two angel-monks) that he is no longer there.

For a long time, you thought of this story of a dematerialized body and some singing Mary-monks and angel-monk(s) as an incredibly entertaining tale of how theatre naturally reemerged in the West as a campy musical theatre drag show played in a pious key. The proto-music-drama takes the dramatic form of a question, a misapprehension, a proclamation, and an action:

ANGEL:	Whom seek ye in the sepulchri, O followers of Christ?
MARYS:	Jesus of Nazareth, who was crucified, O heavenly one.
ANGEL:	He is not here; he is risen, just as he foretold. Go, announce that he is risen from the sepulcher.
MARYS:	Alleluia! (Fraser 1976: 3)

Time and space work differently on this planet. People hear voices on this planet. Things you thought to be true about yourself and the world are no longer true, maybe about yourself, but definitely about the world. Sound familiar?

You digress.

These lines are part of a song that is never written down, never even authorized by the church, yet dozens, maybe even hundreds of versions appear throughout Europe, growing not like tree roots, but like grassroots. The song appears in simultaneous locations, and each time it lands, it *re*makes itself to suit the rhythms and cadence and tempo of that location, though, this is, of course, a guess.

Nevertheless, everywhere the people sing this song, no matter the time signature, they sing the question of what do with a love that never dies. Yes, of course, if you think about it literally this breaks down. But theatre is love and love is theatre, isn't it? People across a continent perform the mystery of how you make that love flesh again and seeing that the best way of making love live is to dress the flesh in theatre, they do so.

If you are the stories you tell yourself, the reemergence of theatre in the West is one of the greatest love stories ever told.

✳✳✳

Yes, you do know that this is a slightly romantic reading of theatre's return, maybe even operatic. But if something returns from the dead, and tells you that it, or they, or *whatever*, never died because they love you that much, this *is* the stuff of opera.

You wonder if medieval people have a feeling of some kind that this song will give birth to theatre. Come to think of it, maybe even opera, and perhaps to cinema, which is, you must agree, the best medium for animating the once dead and making them live again in another way.

On second thought, what you are really wondering about is if the song itself, with no time signature, that is barely even a song, knows that it is dreaming its future ancestors into being. Does it know its own *mystery*?

Let's return to the question of genre you say (without pausing for an answer).

This religious chant, or play, or whatever it is, is certainly in the middle of ritual and theatre, and certainly between sound and music, too, and of course, it tells the story of what it is to be between death and resurrection. It is homeless, you think, no longer here or there but somewhere in between. And though you can say that this song, never written down and only made present when chanted by the singers, is an embodiment of radical change, it is also terrible, this homelessness, this mixed reality, this not knowing where you belong, or in what reality you might find belonging.

It is unclear if you are still talking about Jesus.

Radical change can feel like radical grief, and returns you, me, us, you say, to the question of what it means to be alive differently?

Noli me tangere, you begin without much warning.

The translation, is something like "do not touch me," or "you must let go of me," or "stop clinging to me." You say it is the title of the image painted by innumerable artists over the past millennium depicting the moment Jesus appears to Mary Magdalene in the form of a gardener after his physical death.[1]

In the painted versions, there is only one Mary present, and she is trying to feel her way into this reality by reaching out her hands. John's Gospel tells this story like this:

She turned around and saw Jesus standing there, but she did not realize that it was Jesus. He asked her, "Woman, why are you crying? Who is it you are looking for?" Thinking he was the gardener, she said, "Sir, if you have carried him away, tell me where you have put him, and I will get him." Jesus said to her, "Mary." She turned toward him and cried out in Aramaic, "Rabboni!" (which means "Teacher"). Jesus said, "Do not hold on to me, for I have not yet ascended to the Father. Go instead to my brothers and tell them, 'I am ascending to my Father and your Father, to my God and your God.'" Mary Magdalene went to the disciples with the news: "I have seen the Lord!" And she told them that he had said these things to her. (John 20:14–18)

Dramatically speaking, this is a story of *mis*recognition. Based on the account of their meeting in the biblical passage, Mary never sees Christ in the way we typically understand that action. It is when Jesus *calls* out her name, "Mary," that she turns around and *sees* him as her Rabboni, or Teacher. She sees Christ when he calls her name. When his voice reaches her ears, she immediately reaches out her hands to touch him, greet him, possibly embrace him, as if to say, *Thank god you are still here—What I think is happening is just a dream, and you are still here*. Jesus is in a liminal space between worlds, but, remarkably, Mary can negotiate her way into this mysterious world by seeing with her ears.

Let's be clear here, this is not a story of seeing and believing because nothing about these medieval paintings suggest that what is happening takes place in some ordinary garden. Check out the paintings of this scene by Giotto, or the Lehman Master, or Fra Angelico (see Figures 2.1 to 2.3), and you find images of Jesus and Mary hovering over cliffs, or trees the size of their hands, or angels larger than mountains, and possibly, in Fra Angelico, stigmata from Christ's body peppered across the garden landscape. Or, at least, that is how one famous art historian interprets the painting, and you agree.[2]

Figure 2.1. Giotto di Bondone, *Scenes from the Life of Mary Magdalen: Noli me tangere*, Fresco, Magdalen Chapel, Lower Church, San Francesco, Assisi, Italy, *c.* 1320s.

What you're getting at is that you are not in the world you think you know. Or you are not in the world in the way you think you know it.

This is what you imagine those Sufis call the eighth climate, or no-where. That world that is as real as the world of the senses and the world of the intellect that you must enter through a precise mode of perception. So, what you are trying to understand about these paintings, or what you think might be forcing you to return to them, again, and again, is the question of whether they are really in the garden or whether the garden is actually in *them*. Are these figures and this garden like a Möbius strip, where inside and outside, spiritual and physical life are always already turning into each other? And, if the garden is in them, where are they and where is the garden?[3]

It is not that the paintings simply depict the mystery, but they are painted as a mystery. It is a mixed reality where two-dimensional flatness signals immersion with a virtual world, sort of like in those

Figure 2.2. Lehman Master, *Noli me tangere*, c. fourteenth century. Courtesy of Universal History Archive/Universal Images Group via Getty Images.

Figure 2.3. Fra Angelica, *Noli me tangere*, fresco on the wall of Cell 1 of the Convento di San Marco, Florence, Italy, *c.* 1440–2.

Buddhist thangkas, where Green Tara, or Medicine Buddha (see Figures 2.4 and 2.5) float in a mandala sea of pattern and color. And while this is interesting when it is Green Tara, or Jesus, even, they are already somewhere else. This is really Mary's mystery, and this is what

Figure 2.4. Tibetan thangka painting of Green Tara, *c.* thirteenth century.

preoccupies you, and what you find so devastating. Is there anything more confusing or ungrounding or unsettling, or all three, than a human who unexpectedly finds herself in a mixed reality?

It is unclear if you are still talking about Mary.

This experience is life changing, and maybe for the better, but you do not know this to be true. What if, in some real way, she lives in a mixed reality the rest of her life, and what if, in some real way, no

Figure 2.5. Painted banner (thangka) with the Medicine Buddha (Bhaishajyaguru), c. 1201–1400. Kate S. Buckingham Fund, Art Institute of Chicago.

one else is living in this reality with her? She reaches out her hands because she just wants to know that the person she loves most in the world, the one person who really gets her, is still with her, is still by her side, and Jesus refuses.[4] Sure, maybe he must refuse. Who the hell knows what it is like to be already dead and not-dead? Except, of course, Jesus knows, presumably.

You remain haunted by Mary's outstretched hands, her longing to connect with this figure who is all that her heart desires, to place her hand in his. The mixed reality of the moment does not allow her to fully feel that her sentient hands will never reach him. This gesture of two hands folding into one, a gesture so fully human that it is almost unremarkable except for the clarity of Mary's desire that Christ can only validate by way of a visual refusal is a gesture, Heidegger tells us, that is meant to carry us all "into the great oneness" (1968: 16).

Notes

1 For a great account of the multiple historical renderings of the *Noli me tangere*, see Barbara Baert (2011).
2 See Didi-Huberman (1995).
3 Georges Didi-Huberman (1995) helpfully illuminates how we might think of this intermediate world in the materiality of the painted image. He is frustrated by traditional interpretations professed by art historians who think of the place or location depicted in a painting as mere "background." In discussing Fra Angelico's *Noli me tangere* (1442), he cites Albertus Magnus (1200–1280), a Dominican priest from Cologne who was vehemently opposed to interpretations that conceived of place as mere context. Instead, he suggested that in the paintings in San Marco, Italy (of which the *Noli me tangere* is one) figures do not inhabit a place; they are *produced* by a place. The place exists, for Magnus, as the "power of matter" desiring to manifest as form (1995: 18). "What is at issue here," writes Didi-Huberman, "is precisely a perpetual invocation of visual thinking as a way of moving toward a world of nonvisual thinking that is theological in nature" (1995: 22–3).
4 Jean-Luc Nancy (1998), in writing about Titian's *Noli me tangere* (c. 1514), says that "everything seems arranged to start with the hands and come back to them; in effect, these hands are the gestures and the signs of the intrigue of an arrival (that of Mary) and a departure (that of

Jesus)" (1998: 32). He writes, "we are certain that he will not take hold of her, that he will not even take her hands in his. If he greets her with her name and makes a gift of his appearance to her, it is not to keep her but to send her to announce the news" (1998: 32).

Elizabeth Robertson (2013) exploring the *Noli me tangere* of the Lehman Master through the prism of sensation writes,

> While Mary is prohibited from touching, she comes to acknowledge the figure before her as Christ because, as the theologians assert, she stands for faith. ... The fresco presents not only a desiring subject but also a perceiving one, that is, one who evokes consideration of the nature of human consciousness itself. ... Mary Magdalene's reach in the Lehman fresco, as in all the works in which she appears, epitomizes the condition of the human subject as defined by a desire to reach beyond its limits by reaching out to encounter the world beyond itself through the senses. Her encounter with Christ dramatizes the limits of human sensual knowledge at the same time that it affirms the power of an *inner intuitive knowledge*. [My emphasis; 2013: 44–5)

Lecture 3

Gesture

Ask any young acting student about the difficulties of their craft and they will inevitably say that the question of what to do with their hands is a perennial problem. You tell me that your own students discuss this with you, but the challenge precedes them by decades, if not centuries. Konstantin Stanislavski (1863–1938), the famous Russian director and acting teacher, writes about how his own students devalue the hands in his *An Actor Prepares* ([1936] 2013). Written in the form of a diary of a fictional acting student in his first year of training in Stanislavski's system of acting, the teacher returns again and again to the relationship between the hands and the imagination.

Tortsov, the name of the fictional acting teacher, tries to convey the importance of small gestures by recalling for his students how Lady Macbeth—at the culminating point in her tragedy—is preoccupied with washing a spot of blood on her hand. A student in his class thinks it is ridiculous to suggest that Shakespeare wrote this tragedy to focus our attention on the simple gesture of Lady Macbeth washing her hands.

You forgive the student's inability to put aside grandeur for the reality of such a quotidian act, or, as Tortsov lectures his student, "in real life many great moments of emotion are signaled by some ordinary small, natural movement" (Stanislavski 2013: 129). The student is young and knows little about mortality, which is what Tortsov tries to convey as he turns from a discussion of this Shakespearean scene to the scene of an imagined loved one who is dying.

He asks the student to consider the activities in which a friend or relative of a loved one might keep themselves occupied while their beloved is dying. Preserving quiet in the room, he suggests, or carrying out the doctor's orders, taking the temperature, applying compression, he continues.

You're surprised that he yokes these two experiences together. You never notice the ways that your own associations with how hands bring theatre and death into conversation are tacitly linked by Stanislavski. Once you see it, you can't unsee it, and you can't unsee its relationship to that medieval painting you keep going on about.

Tortsov, for his part, has the student's hands bandaged when he begins using them too freely in his acting scene. When asked why he does this, Tortsov replies, "I want you to be convinced that whereas the eyes are the mirror of the soul, the tips of the fingers are the eyes of the body" (Stanislavski 2013: 181).

You recall the scene of Mary reaching out her hands and Jesus's resistance to touch and you think it is possible that Jesus might be Mary's first acting teacher. There's something about the way he tells her *you don't need your hands for this, reality in the way you understand it is not a part of this scene right now, we're here together resting in an internal garden that doesn't require your hands to act.*

Mary, he might have continued, *let's think about this moment: what we've got here is a failure of the imagination to render real that which we cannot touch. If you can't do that, how do you expect others to believe?*

You yourself have spent most of your adult lifetime trying to convey the reality of the imaginal world to students who are told repeatedly that after they leave this training ground, they will have to forgo these questions to enter *the real world*. But if the real world isn't where you are, where have you been your whole life? Reality is a sticking point for you, or is, at least, sticky, so you can't dismiss the issue: what is the real world? You suspect that, like Mary finally understands, most of what is real in the world you can't actually touch.

You also suspect that you learn this from Eleonora Duse (1858–1924). An Italian tragedienne and the first modern actor in the Western world. You are certain she would agree about Jesus being Mary's acting teacher. If anyone understands how theatre takes us into the mystery, it is Duse. She understands the grandeur of a small, silent gesture.

In your office, sometime later, you show me the newspaper clippings that you find in the Eleonora Duse archive[1]—a glimpse at the source of what is now largely understood as the basis of Stanislavski's entire system of actor training:[2]

> "But Mme. Duse's most wonderful possessions are her arms and hands, with which she points her speeches in a way which defies all, but her hands never seem to lose their tension or become tender and caressing. They grasp when they might touch, and clutch instead of hold.
>
> —1893 (?), [unidentified author], "Eleanor [sic Eleonora] Duse Without Artificial Glamour," *New York Herald*
>
> There was the old exquisite play of the hands, that constant fumbling and gathering of her dress which, as in a statue, it becomes part of the body's interpretation as with Duse the body becomes the soul.
>
> —1923, [unidentified author], "Duse in 'The Lady from the Sea.'" *The Manchester Guardian* (London), June 8
>
> Poets and critics have made famous the beauty of her expressive hands. ... how she smiles with them, pleads with them, confuses with them! It is as though she had an extra keyboard for the expression of emotion, her voice, her face—and her hands.
>
> —1928 Desmond McCarthy, "Drama," *The New Statesman*, June 16
>
> And watch her beautiful hands as they flutter about in minor gestures and sweep the air when power and strength are required. They are a poem, so exquisite are they in themselves and so purposeful in their use.

—1924, George C. Warren, "Duse Superb as Blind Wife in Tragic Drama," review of Duse in Gabriel D'Annunzio's *The Dead City* [unidentified source], March 14

Duse's name will live as the supreme argument for gentleness. … But superlatives of praise elude her, for her art was a protest against superlatives in acting. She had no flourish and did not soar to conquer. With a pass of her hands, she walked into our hearts.

—Ivor Brown (1926: 192-3), *Masques and Phases*

Included in these notes is a photograph of a plaster cast of Eleonora Duse's right hand. (Figure 3.1).

***

The photograph of Duse's plaster hand haunts you. You find reference to it in several museum collections. There is evidence of a prolific number of her hands circulating the Atlantic world. The plaster hands

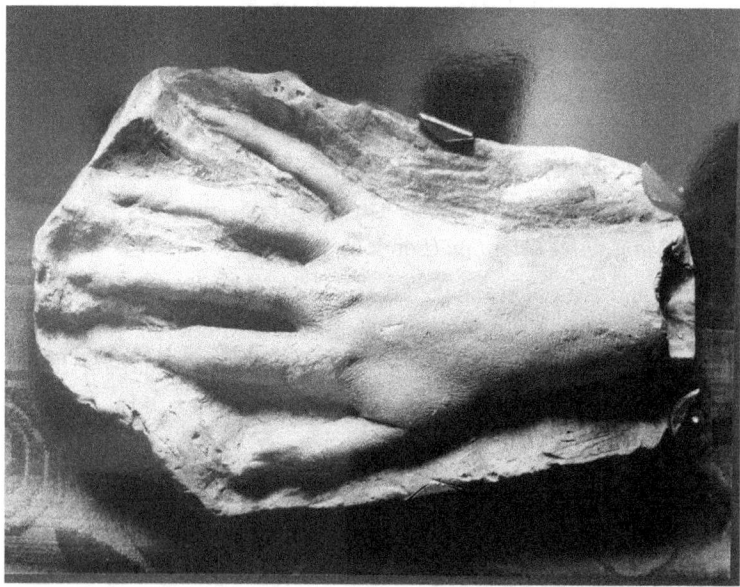

Figure 3.1. Photograph of plaster cast of Eleonora Duse's right hand taken by author.

remind you of medieval relics in the age of mechanical reproduction. What is it that the medieval people are after when they decide to take bits of a saint's body—bits of their clothes, or hair, or fingernails, or maybe even a whole finger, or hand? And what are they after when they worship religious icons, which some scholars suggest are understood as having a life force.[3] Is it the same thing that Duse's fans are after as they look for ways of worshiping their icon? An icon made present in the material form of a plaster cast of her hand? And what are *you* doing in her archive about one hundred years later, taking digital pictures of a photograph that could itself be a copy of a photograph, of a plaster cast, that is a copy of a hand, but not *the* copy. It is a copy of a copy of copy. And is the photograph that you find in the archive waiting for *you* to take that digital picture? Does this iconic image have a life force of its own? Is this Duse-drenched icon in the age of mechanical reproduction waiting for a future audience member to put time back in the image, to keep it in motion?

You tell me that all these questions are really a way of asking: What does it mean for an image to survive its own death? Or what does it mean for an image to have an afterlife? Is it possible, you wonder, for a gesture to be frozen in an image, left there for hundreds of years, and quite without precedent, be activated in another medium through the living gestures of a different kind of mystic who also has the power to see with her ears, a power made visible in the image of her hands?[4]

Whether it is Mary's hands or Duse's hands, both are longing for a glimpse of reality, what Duse calls in a letter to her daughter, Enrichetta, as "Life itself, and it is *outside* of life" (qtd in Weaver 1984: 301). In some inexplicable and undeniable way, you reanimate the gesture from her archive, connect with the energy of the quest through your own kind of performance. Duse's hand is not *the* Reality, but it points you in the right direction. You tell me that you now feel like Mary—trying to reach Duse on the other side of the rift through a desire to make contact with her (now plaster) hands. You say that she leaves them circulating the world so that someone might take them and be carried away from the stage, might disappear into that other Reality for which the stage is a mere veil. Even you cannot imagine where she sends you once she realizes that you are serious about seeking out Reality, that you want to find this Life "outside of life."

Though you are slightly tentative about admitting this, you tell me that not too long ago you seek the support of a career counselor because you, yourself, no longer feel you are in the right story. You feel you are being called to a different life, still feel this, but you lack the imagination to bring this life into reality, or even imagine what world might want to be built.

The career counselor suggests that you bring in a series of action steps to help you investigate different options. Like Aristotle, she seems to know that action comes before character. It is completely ludicrous that one of the main action steps on your list, the one you're most excited to enact, is to attend a conference in Florida you discover on the internet the previous day: The Afterlife Awareness Conference. In this space, the space of a hotel in this instance, hospice doctors, nurses, energy workers, shamans, mystics, and mediums gather to give lectures on the different ways that they research, explore, and experience something called the afterlife.

Months later you attend the conference despite your anxiety about what this decision says about your character. You tell me that you attend countless theatre conferences over the years where people give talks on some pale approximation of the imaginal world, but this is the first conference you attend where the speakers actually believe the imaginal world is Real. If you're honest, it feels like a relief. This tension between your career in the theatre and where the medium of theatre leads you has Duse's fingerprints all over it.

You know this first when you sign up for an introductory workshop on mediumship. The teacher takes you through a series of exercises that are helpful for sharpening intuition. The exercises would be familiar to you from improvisation class, or the object is similar anyway: to bypass the rational mind so that you begin to work in alignment with instinct. There is certainly not an exercise that you practice that is unfamiliar to artists attempting to access creative dimensions. Not for the first time, you understand that Duse is a medium between two worlds. But this still does not explain how her hands got you here.

While there are more shamans, mediums, and mystics gathered inside the hotel than is prudent, these are not the people you find the most curious. Instead, you keep bumping into and befriending hospice nurses, and women who call themselves end-of-life doulas. You hear about these doulas just before attending the conference, and then continue to read everything you can find, but this, too, is curious. You are surprised that you have such an appetite for death and dying, and an even greater appetite for this thing called afterlife. You wonder if this why Duse dies over and over on the stage. Why she is best known for tragedy. Is it because she, too, has an appetite for death and dying? You tell me that you've pieced together some notes on Duse to find a way into the mystery you both share.

***

The Age of Duse: Notes for a Performative Lecture

I go on a ten-day silent meditation retreat. I return. A friend asks me what it was like. I say that if I was an actress, it would be a great way to prepare for a part. He asks, "why?" I say, "when you meditate for that long, parts of you disappear—there's less 'you' to get in the way, more space for something else to come in" (that's a guess; I'm not an actor). He asks, "have you ever read *The Mystic in the Theatre*?" I say "no," and then I read it. It's about the life of Eleonora Duse (1858–1924).

She meditated. I also learn that Duse and I are interested in the same medieval mystics.[5]

In the archive I become obsessed with her hands. It's not hard to see why. Everyone was obsessed with them. But critics and audiences had actually seen them, or were transported by them, or healed by them, or felt heard by them. What was it, exactly? And now I'm wearing an archivist's white gloves and taking digital pictures of a photograph of a plaster cast of Eleonora Duse's right hand.

She was an Italian tragedienne. She was the first modern actor in the Western world. She played the transitions, acted between the words (most often the words of terribly written plays). She was not afraid of silence. She was said to shape-shift before audiences. By all accounts, she was a shaman. Duse's superpower was her ability to disappear, leaving only her plaster hands as evidence that she was a material presence in the world. Disappearance. Reproduction. She knew the theatrical drill.

She leaves the stage in 1909. "To save the theatre, the theatre must be destroyed," she says in 1912 (qtd in Symons 1927: 3).

May 1915: Italy enters World War I. Duse refuses to entertain the troupes on the frontlines. She goes instead to sit with the soldiers—writing letters for them, holding their hands, delivering packages, listening. She stays in a hotel close to the warfare during one visit. When she returns, her hotel is a pile of rubble. Bombed. Her timing was always impeccable.

Letter dated December 15, 1915, to Enrichetta, her daughter in England whom we now have evidence was a British spy. "I have done everything in life between one departure and another—the heart has remained motionless, turned toward that suffering, that light, that thing that is everything and that is nothing" (qtd in Weaver 1984: 301).

This is what I am after, I think, as I follow her hands. Evidence of where theatre is really taking us, has always taken us.

Duse studies the new cinema, or "silent medium" (her term): "All is seen, experienced: documents, evidence in hand—a news item. The exterior of a poor life, displayed by machine, every evening the same way. Nothing of what is not seen and weaves a life" (qtd in Weaver 1984: 305). The first moving images on cinema screens during World War I display a terrifying number of corpses, sentient and celluloid. What to do with all of those missing bodies?

To Enrichetta, June 1916, "the realization of film is a spiritual problem" (qtd in Pagani 2017: 94).

Medieval art is the answer to her spiritual problem. Another language for connecting with missing bodies (?). 1916, Duse films *Cenere* (*Ashes*). She treats filmic images like tableaux vivant, living pictures (or corpse pose?). Duccio's "Descent from the Cross" (c. 1308–1311) and Giotto's "Lamentation" (1306) find their way into the film (Sica & Wilson 2012: 92).

We teach students that theatre is reborn in the churches of medieval Europe. For all we know, it is reborn a thousand times in a thousand places during those pesky "Dark Ages." This time, though, theatre is reborn through a popular musical number about a missing body. "Whom do you seek?" the angel sings to the Marys. "Where's Jesus?" they sing back. "He's where he said he would be: not here, but not *not* here," the angel belts out before telling them to spread the good news.

Disappearance. Reappearance. Disappearance. Reappearance. This death does history like theatre. Duse patiently wrings the very life out of the dusty tragedies she performs to play with a death like this. When she does, her audiences follow her hands all the way to oblivion. "Life is not cinema," she writes to Giorgio Papini (qtd in Vacche 2008: 138). Neither is death.[6]

In 1918, Duse tests positive for the "Spanish Flu." (Federico Garcia Lorca later writes of her *duende*, play and death her forte.[7]) She survives and returns to her plays in 1922. She needs the money. The theatre had not died, but it most definitely kills her.

April 1924: Outside in the rain, unable to get in through the locked stage door. Drenched. First influenza. Then pneumonia. She dies at age 65. In Pittsburgh. She is performing Marco Praga's *La Porta Chiusa*, or *The Closed Door*. Play and Death.

To Enrichetta, 1917, "You who live in a high intellectual environment, do not believe that your mother follows the Church, or chooses the Middle Ages just because I have chosen something from the thirteenth century. Not at all. On the contrary, it is very modern, as everything recurs, wars, illnesses, beauty and ugliness, greatness and the stupidity of the world" (qtd in Sica & Wilson, 2012: 97) .

***

In 1909, at the age of fifty, Duse quits the theatre and begins to conduct her own research in recurrence by using silent film to recompose medieval paintings. You think back to her only film, produced in 1916, at the height of World War I, and one whose name evokes the pathos of the time: *Cenere (Ashes)*, an adaptation of Grazia Deledda's 1904 novel. The story—which is an amalgam of all the *mater dolorosa* roles made famous by Duse in the theatre— gives us the life of Rosalia, a single mother in poverty forced to entrust her child to her lover, married to another woman. The little boy, once an adult, finds his real mother and wants to establish a relationship, but his future wife refuses her. To spare her child the difficult decision of choosing between his wife and his mother, she commits suicide.

In the film, when Duse's character dies and is laid to rest, she creates a kind of mixed tableaux inspired by Giotto's "Lamentation" (1304–6) and Duccio's "Descent from the Cross" (*c*. 1308–11; see Figures 3.2 and 3.3). What feels important is how Duse manages to make these images so personal, how she uses them to tell a human story of love, betrayal, heartbreak, suffering, and death—not because God wills it (as in the Jesus story), but because of the stupidity of the world.

Figure 3.2. Giotto di Bondone, *Lamentation* (*The Mourning of Christ*), Scrovegni Chapel, Padua, Italy, c. 1304–6.

It is in the film's death scene where Duse immerses herself into these medieval images. She doesn't so much evoke her own personal Jesus as much as she *becomes* her own personal Jesus. As you follow her death through multiple camera shots, you see that she is literally in the place of the crucified Christ in the medieval paintings she recomposes (see Figure 3.4). The details do not need to be an exact fit, it is the flavor of medieval pathos that she is after. It is not *his* suffering that is important, but the way her character's suffering is now one with those suffering images.

In returning to those medieval images, she inadvertently returns to a medieval sensibility that does not think of the self, or personhood,

Figure 3.3. Duccio, *Descent from the Cross*, Museo dell'Opera del Duomo, Siena, Italy, *c.* 1308–11.

as having boundaries, but instead thinks of personhood in a way that echoes Barbara Newman's "permeable self" in medieval life. You recall Newman explaining that "the essence of personhood is the capacity to be permeated by other selves, other persons, without being fractured by them." In this paradigm, "the personal is, by definition, the interpersonal. One cannot be a person by oneself, only with, through, and in other persons" (2021: 6). You wonder if this is why you are so interested in Duse. Her immersion in the story of the Passion is reminding you of your immersion in this story, *and* in her story—the way you pay careful attention to the moment she quits the theatre in 1909.

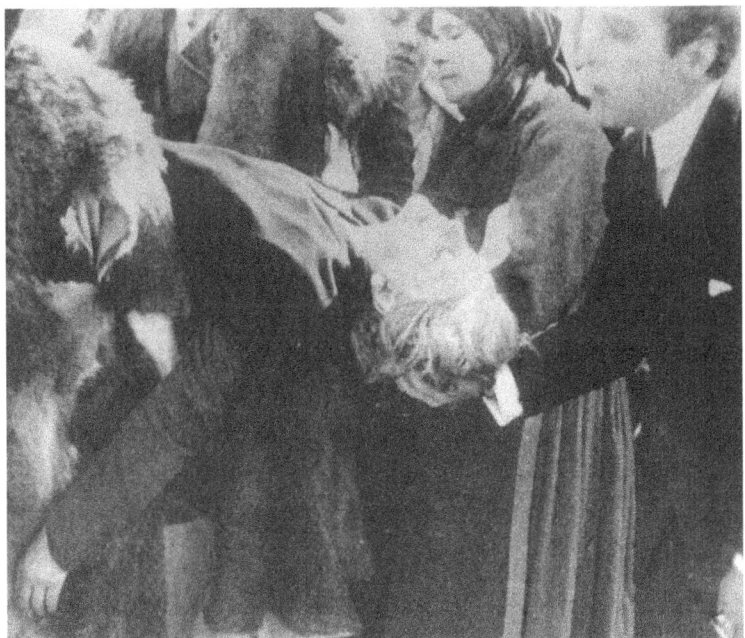

Figure 3.4. Film still of Eleonora Duse playing Rosalia Derios in *Cenere*, dir. Fabo Mari, Ambrosio Film Company, Italy, 1916.

Is her departure from theatre at the age of fifty unconsciously signaling the question of what you will become once you leave the discipline of theatre at the same age? Is that why you are obsessed with her life once she leaves the theatre? Are you made a person with, through, and even *in* her? You're not certain, but you're surprised by how much you feel her with you as each year passes. It is as if she is always here in some timeless present tense.

You recall the highly popular meditation techniques recorded in Ludolph of Saxony's *Vita Christi* completed in 1374 because he, too, uses the idea of immersion effectively. In the prologue to his influential text, he tells the reader to use the Bible like a memory atlas. "Although these Biblical accounts describe events that occurred in the past," he begins, "you must meditate upon them as if they were taking place now: there is no question but that you will savor them with greater pleasure. Read what once happened as if it were happening here and now. Put past deeds before your eyes as if they were present; you will experience them more discreetly and more happily" (Walsh 2011: 34).

This text is so popular that, over one hundred years later, when Ignatius of Loyola is convalescing during an illness, he is given Ludolph's text. Taking Ludolph's ideas one step further, Ignatius tells his readers to become avatars in a virtual reality: "Come and be present at his birth, and his circumcision, like a good foster parent with Joseph. Likewise come with the magi to Bethlehem, and worship the young King with them," writes Ignatius. "Be present at his death with his blessed mother and John and share in their suffering and consolation" (Shore 1998: 17).

You digress. Your point, if you have one, is that strictly speaking, whatever is happening when Duse transposes medieval paintings into her film, or in the immersive meditation techniques of Ludolph of Saxony or Ignatius of Loyola, this is never really about Jesus. Newman writes that "the permeable self appears most often at the liminal junctures and imagined end points of personal history" (2021: 8). Once you let go of the strong hold of biography being destiny, the medieval sense of interpersonal selfhood suggests that something more mysterious emerges.

What might be most mysterious, at least for you, is how similar these immersive techniques are to Konstantin Stanislavski's theory of building a character by using a process he calls the "magic if" or "as if" (i.e., *What would I do if I were in this situation? How would I respond if I found myself facing these problems? What thoughts would go through my head if that happened to someone I loved?*). Taking a note from Ludolph of Saxony who tells his readers to meditate on a scene *as if* it was happening now, all the way through Ignatius of Loyola who tells his readers simply to be present at the event in question (there is, apparently, no longer a need to even imagine; one can just *be present*), the permeable self appears in that liminal space between actor and character, between self and other, where you are not sure where one ends and the other begins. Closely related to the permeable self, Newman writes, "is the boundary between consciousness and performance—the inward, reflective dimension of the self and its outward, theatrical aspect" (2021: 8). Another way of thinking about this porous boundary between inner and outer is *gesture*—that which links psyche to soma—which is, of course, Duse's stock-in-trade.

This is what confuses you for a long time. You tell me that there is a paradox in an actress whose use of gesture in the theatre is so celebrated that people write poems about her beautiful hands, while her use of gesture in film is more contradictory in the way it both amplifies and splits the relationship between inner and outer self. When Duse first sees herself on film, she finds the way the screen amplifies her gestures both liberating and alienating. You think that her excitement with gesture is tied to her role as an actress. For Duse, the "silent medium" of film has the capacity to create a universal language through gesture. In *Cenere*, she is proud that she never once opens her mouth, but simply moves her head to indicate 'yes' or 'no'; otherwise, she communicates with her hands (see Pagani 2018).

Her role as director—as the one who is watching the actress—is more invested in things like the transposition of medieval images into the final death scene in the film. Here she wishes for audiences to see in the final images an echo of the earlier images of suffering, and, in some oblique way, a commentary. Bertolt Brecht (1898–1956), the German theatre pioneer who made famous the idea of the alienation-effect in theatre, is only eighteen years old when Duse makes her only film. Yet, you cannot help thinking that Duse's excitement for the amplification of gesture in film unwittingly echoes Brecht's understanding of *social gestus*—a heightened gesture that works to break the connection between inner self and exterior expression and alienates it from everyday life. Fredric Jameson describes *Gestus* as "a whole process, in which a specific act—indeed a particular event, situated in time and space, and affiliated with specific concrete individuals—is then somehow identified and renamed, associated with a larger and more abstract type of action in general, transformed into something exemplary" (Jameson 1998: 103).

You are certain that Duse, the actress, would find Brecht's ideas about alienation anathema (her beautiful hands and the plaster casts made of them would hardly be celebrated if she had lost control of the naturalistic language of gesture). You are less certain as to whether Duse, the director, feels the same way. For Brecht, *gestus* allows for critical distance between actor and character, so that audiences can reflect on what they are watching, see it as less inevitable, which can lead them toward a changed relationship with representation and, therefore, with reality. In Duse's role as director, her demands, like Brecht's directorial demands, exceed claims to naturalism (exasperating her producer and co-director in the process): she refuses close-ups, never wears makeup, never hides her age, never pretends to speak, and, of course, works diligently to transpose those medieval images into her own idiom. Her commentary may not be Brechtian, but she is certainly making a claim for a different understanding of reality—transforming her gestures into something "exemplary."

You think about the way that the dead Duse in *Cenere* is immersed in the image of the dead Jesus, which is also the story of being alive in another way, or, if not completely alive, then in some liminal space. Her acting, like her death on screen where the town's people carry her out of the shot, is always working in that liminal space where binaries collapse, where the self becomes porous, and you are left with the eternal question about whether you ever really die or if the absent body is just the beginning of the story. Duse often wrote in letters to her friends about the oblivion that befalls the art of the actress after her death—how the actor's art simply disappears. You recall her letter to Giorgio Papini where she complains that "life is not cinema," and you wonder if Duse knows that *Cenere*, recorded in a medium that she ultimately finds so alienating, is also the record of her afterlife.

Notes

1. All newspaper clippings are in the Eleonora Duse Collection, MS Gen 1659, University of Glasgow Special Collections, Glasgow, Scotland. <https://www.gla.ac.uk/myglasgow/archivespecialcollections/discover/specialcollectionsa-z/eleonoradusecollection/> accessed June 19, 2023. For further details, search item title in References.
2. While the enormity of Duse's influence is little known outside of actor-training circles, there are very few adjectives one can use that do justice to her legacy. In a speech given after one of Duse's performances in Moscow by influential Russian theatre maker Konstantin Stanislavski (1863–1938), he said that he "got his inspiration for founding the Moscow Art Theatre from witnessing a performance of Duse's," and that "not a rehearsal of the company had ever gone by without referring to her or her art" (Sheehy 2003: 248). Stanislavski's system of acting serves as the foundation for the method acting developed by America's most influential acting teachers: Lee Strasberg, Stella Adler, and Sanford Meisner. Without exaggeration, everything we see in Hollywood film today has been influenced by these three teachers, who were influenced by Stanislavski, who based his system on the work of Eleonora Duse.
3. Writing about the life force of icons, Hans Belting (1994) tells this story:

> A few years ago the Venetians celebrated the return of the Virgin *Nicopeia* to S. Marco, from which it had been forcibly removed. In the old republic the icon had been publicly honoured as the true sovereign of the state. The prehistory of its cult in Venice leads back to Byzantium, where in 1203 the icon was seized from the chariot of the opposing general. For the Byzantines it was the embodiment of their celestial commander, to whom the emperors gave precedence at victory celebrations. The Venetians took home this palladium, which they gained as a fruit of victory and which in turn brought them victory, as a part of the "transfer of cults." They placed their

community under the icon's protection just as the ancient Greeks had once done with Athena from Troy. The icon was soon known in Venice as St. Luke's Madonna. ... It led a unique existence, even a life of its own. At state ceremonies, it was received as if it were an actual person. The image, as object, demanded protection, just as it in turn granted protection as an agent of the one whom it depicted. (1994: 4)

4 This line of questioning is inspired by Aby Warburg's (1866–1929) concept of "survivals" in art history, which is also the subject of Georges Didi-Huberman's (2017) *The Surviving Image: Phantoms of Time and Time of Phantoms—Aby Warburg's History of Art*.

5 In Le Gallienne's (1899–1991) *Mystic in the Theatre* (1965), she recounts how she once found Duse sitting in a chair facing a corner in her room where she sat for hours. When asked what she was doing, Duse said she was "in prayer... I'm trying to forget myself—to free myself from myself ... That way, perhaps, I won't be so afraid" (1965: 111). Later in the narrative, Le Gallienne explains how "this power of 'one-pointed' concentration—of action through inaction—was the foundation of that discipline of the spirit which enabled her, to an ever greater extent as she developed as an artist, to eliminate self, and become a clear channel for that higher force it was her aim to serve" (1965: 163). Throughout the book we also hear of Eleonora's sharp intellect and wide-ranging study. I was struck most of all by her study of mysticism, and her love of medieval saints: Teresa of Avila, St. John of the Cross, and Francis of Assisi, to name a few. Yet, her interest did not stop at the doors of the church. She read books on Chinese and Indian mysticism, and in a letter written to her daughter, Enrichetta, in 1915, she asked, "Tell me in which volume Renan speaks of Gotama [sic] Buddha, I don't have my books with me" (Duse qtd in Weaver 1984: 300).

6 Her first and only film *Cenere* (*Ashes*), based on the novel by Grazia Deledda, premiered in 1916. William Weaver (1984), one of Duse's biographers, tells us that in 1914 Duse became an "assiduous movie-goer," frequently going to the cinema to study the medium. What she discovered during her cinematic research trips is that "the realization of film is a spiritual problem," as she wrote to her daughter shortly before shooting *Cenere* in June 1916.

Wanting to see how Sardou's *Odette*, once a play in her own repertoire and now a silent film, "would make the journey from *word* to *cinema*," she wrote an exasperating review in a letter to her cinema enthusiast friend, Giorgio Papini. Discussing the last act where "the sailors who found the body in the water asked where they should carry the poor dead woman," Duse writes that in the play she said: "Here—receive her in this house, I beg you" (Weaver 1984: 305). These "*few* and *clear*" words, Duse writes, are sufficient when spoken with "(theatrical weapon) emotion. To say them, one minute suffices." After setting up the scene using theatre's dramaturgical tool kit, she goes in for the punch:

> an hour or more of cinema to illustrate all of this. Here, you *see*. Here there are *actions*, not *words*. It's all here: the sea, the wind, the boat, the sail, and the woman—the woman with hat and veil, then without a hat or veil any more, but with "*with desperation*" (says the title that explains)—*You see everything*. [...] There's everything—all is seen, experienced: documents, evidence in hand—a news item. The exterior of a poor life, displayed by machine, every evening the same way. Trash—shame! And nothing that stimulates the soul—nothing that, after the word, frees the imagination!—Nothing of what is *not* seen and weaves life; nothing of the inevitabilities that form it, that grip it in a vise—In a word: what I saw is not art—I was so worn out and fed up! And who is right? They, or I? ... (Weaver 1984: 305–6)

For Duse, the challenge of moving from theatre to cinema is not that the actors cannot speak in silent film, although one could be forgiven for thinking in these terms since Duse, herself, charts the journey as one from "*word* to *cinema*." Instead, the issue is that *you see everything*. That Duse went on to make *Cenere* a year after this letter was written means that she did not think the medium was without merit, but that it needed to work less like theatre and more like painting. It could exploit the silence to its advantage. When she did decide to make *Cenere*, she imagined it as a book to be illustrated. It was in the return to medieval characters, moods, and images that Duse thought the unique artistic qualities of the new cinematic medium could best be illustrated.

7 In Federico Garcia Lorca's "Theory and Play of the Duende" ([1933] 2010), he writes, "the *duende* is a force not a labour, a struggle not a thought. I heard an old *maestro* of the guitar say: 'The *duende* is not in the throat: the *duende* surges up, inside, from the soles of the feet.' Meaning, it's not a question of skill, but of a style that's truly alive: meaning, it's in the veins: meaning, it's of the most ancient culture of immediate creation" (2010: 57).

Speaking of Duse, he continues, "often the duende of the composer passes into the duende of the interpreter, and at other times, when a composer or poet is no such thing, the interpreter's duende—this is interesting—creates a new marvel that looks like, but is not, the primitive form. This was the case for Eleonora Duse, possessed by duende, who looked for plays that had failed so she could make them triumph thanks to her own inventions" (2010: 63).

Lecture 4

Alienation

There will always come a time in any meaningful play when you are asked to reflect upon the question: "what changes?" Everything always changes, so this needs to be a rather striking change. It is usually in the middle of the story, but it can really be anywhere the dramatist places it. Wherever it is placed, it asks you to find an essential moment that you must pass through that will take you from the beginning to the end of the play (see Fuchs 2004). Since the OG mystery play (i.e., the *Quem quaeritis* trope) begins in catastrophe, before moving to a reversal of what you know to be true, and ending in recognition,[1] you are guessing that the change in your own real-life mystery play is also a "recognition" of what you know to be true about yourself, but maybe also about the world.

You are mopping your floor one afternoon and listening to an audiobook of Thomas Moore's *A Religion of One's Own* (2015) when he starts discussing an unaligned-agnostic-Jewish-French-Marxist-mystic named Simone Weil (1909–1943).[2] She is convalescing in Assisi (after an accident in Spain where she goes to fight the Fascists; the accident, which involves her spilling hot oil, is blamed on her notoriously clumsy hands). Anyway, she is in Assisi and visits *La Porziuncola*, St. Francis's first church, says Moore. She is standing there in that little twelfth-century Romanesque chapel when all of a sudden she says that something stronger than she is compels her for the first time in her life to go down on her knees. She's overwhelmed.[3]

It is remarkable because at the very moment you hear about her mystical experience, you are looking at a painted tile of the

Annunciation you purchased in Assisi, a replica of the one you saw in *La Porziuncola* years ago because the visit also changed your life (although you didn't fall on your knees). There is also the interesting coincidence that in the Eleonora Duse archive you come across a photograph of Duse's home in Asolo, Italy, that she names *La Porziuncola* after her pilgrimage to Assisi in 1895.

You digress. In your own mystical-madness (it is still not clear which side of the hyphen you occupy), you take Simone Weil's experience in *La Porziuncola* as a sign! You go to the library and find everything Simone Weil writes and everything that is written about her. You do a good job. You open the first book and see that she writes about Pythagoras. In fact, this essay you read answers all the weird questions you ever have about why Pythagoras thinks God and number are the same thing. "There is never anything in human thought but relationships," writes Weil in "The Pythagorean Doctrine" (1957b):

> This identity is what St. John expressed in giving to Christ the name of the relation, *logos*, and what the Pythagoreans express in saying: "All is number." When we know that, we know that we live in divine mediation, not as a fish in the sea but as a drop of water in the sea. In us, outside us, here below, in the Kingdom of God, nowhere is there any other thing. And mediation is exactly the same thing as Love (1957b: 197).

And then you read what she writes about *Antigone* and Greek tragedy.
And then you read what she writes about attention and affliction.
And then you read what everyone has to say about her eating disorder.
And then you read everything you can find about the strange circumstances that led her to dying alone in a tuberculosis sanatorium in Kent, England in 1943.
And then you try to bring more people into your story with her—ancestors, friends, strangers, historical figures. You try to

bring everything into relation. You want to keep it focused on all the things you have in common, all the things that bring you into relationship. Maybe you think this will help her to recognize you. But at some point, you get preoccupied with her death, maybe even a little obsessed with her death. Her death feels like a part of your own story, but you can't really say why. You start to sketch out some notes for a lecture.

***

Simone Weil's Relationships: Lecture Notes

It is her death that gets me. Everyone has something to say about it. Nothing positive. Pretty despicable, really. Self-starvation; willful brat; crazy lady; pious martyr. Yeah, sure, I can see it.

It makes me angry, but so does she, showing up unexpectedly and forcing me to think about her death, death in general.

A therapist friend (who has never heard of her) diagnoses her on the spot when I attempt to explain: "Anorexia."

Simone Weil (1909–1943), mystic, activist, scholar, pacifist, and patron saint of anomalous persons, dies of tuberculosis at Grosvenor Sanatorium in Kent, England, on August 24, 1943. Five months after penicillin is available to the general public, but not for her. Margaret Gough (1864–1943), my great grandmother, dies of tuberculosis three months before Simone. Also, no penicillin. There's a war going on.

"Unaligned mystic," says Thomas Moore; "A saint," says T. S. Eliot; "The only great spirit of our time," says Albert Camus.

"Cardiac failure due to starvation and pulmonary tuberculosis. The deceased did kill and slay herself by refusing to eat whilst the balance of her mind was disturbed," says Weil's death certificate (qtd in Cabaud 1964: 348).

I hope one person is with her when she dies who is not an asshole. Given the death certificate, it is not her doctor.

Tuesday Express headline, 1943: "French professor starves herself to death."

Kent Messenger headline, 1943: "Death from starvation, French professor's curious sacrifice" (qtd in Cabaud 1964: 350).

And, you know, tuberculosis. That old chestnut.[4]

Do you know there were 1.5 million deaths from tuberculosis in 2018? The leading cause of death worldwide.

Airborne disease. Respiratory illness. A global threat.

She dies with no family within 3,000 miles. They are finally safe in New York. She alone ventures back across the Atlantic, to London, with some vague hope of being sent to France to fight in the resistance. A death sentence for a Jewish woman. She is, of course, never sent.[5]

Born in Paris to agnostic Jewish parents, by her teens she masters two dead languages and several living ones. The only uncontested fact about her personality: she's brilliant.

She quits teaching the classics in 1934 to labor in factories around Paris. It's funny, really, how unsuited she is for the work. But it teaches her a lot about affliction, which she says is "the uprooting of life, a more or less attenuated equivalent of death, made irresistibly present to the soul by the attack or immediate apprehension of physical pain" (Weil 2009: 68).

Two years later, she publishes "Antigone" in *Between Ourselves*, a little factory magazine. It's "for the masses," she says (see "Antigone" 1957a). Her article focuses on Uncle-King Creon sentencing Antigone to a living death. He walls her up in a cave to die, unseen, because she gives her brother, deemed an enemy of the state, a proper burial.

The obligation of public mourning, Antigone insists. The right of the state to refuse to acknowledge the dead, Creon demands.

This dead language knows something about the affliction of the powerless and the politics of death.

And speaking of dead languages, I am amazed when Weil explains why Pythagoras thinks God and number are the same thing: "All that is known involves number. For without number nothing can be thought or known" (Weil 1957b: 153). Replace number with God and read again. Pythagorean geometry is all about the connection between the seen and unseen world. She loves the way it brings unalike things into relationship.

But I'm still not sure I understand her because Weil's own mystical logic always swings back and forth, a kind of portal between degrees of consciousness: part science, part something else.

The *part something else* starts to take hold and reminds me that I'm still frustrated by my therapist friend. Her quick diagnosis, "anorexia," plucking out the heart of Weil's mystery. I wake up the morning after we talk, and a name whispers itself in my ear.

Catherine of Siena.

Later I read: mystic, activist, scholar, doctor of the church, Patron Saint of Nurses.

Even later I read: Catherine of Siena (1347–1380) is born in the year of the plague, or Black Death. Estimates show the world's population decreases from 450 million to about 350 million after the plague of 1347 (also, no penicillin). It recurs three times in Catherine's life.

She is only one year younger than Simone's thirty-four years when she dies. Like Simone, she dies in the midst of war and pandemic. And she dies of self-starvation, unable to eat.[6]

Rudolph M. Bell writes in *Holy Anorexia* (1985): "In the end she had committed the sin of vainglory and had starved herself to death. It had been her will, and not His, that had triumphed all these years and that now lay vanquished" (1985: 53). A judge-y death certificate written over 500 years after her death, little better than Simone's own.

And then there is Susan Sontag, bowing before Weil's mystery: "No one who loves life would wish to imitate her dedication to martyrdom nor would wish it for his children nor for anyone else whom he loves.

Yet so far as we love seriousness, as well as life, we are moved by it, nourished by it. In the respect we pay to such lives, we acknowledge the presence of mystery in the world—and mystery is just what the secure possession of the truth, an objective truth, denies" (Sontag 1963).

"Every being cries out silently to be read differently," cries Weil, silently, in one of her notebooks (*Gravity and Grace* [GG] 1952a: 188).

She also says, "The poet produces the beautiful by fixing his attention on something real. It is the same with the act of love. To know that this man who is hungry and thirsty really exists as much as I do—that is enough, the rest follows of itself" (*GG* 1952a: 173).

Catherine knows this love. Hunger is complicated.[7]

By all accounts Catherine is a healer and miracle worker. We are told that "her voice, lovely both in speech and song, soothed dying beds; her touch and prayers healed the sick" (Roberts 1906: 52).

Whether she cures all the sick cannot really be verified. She helps to heal the dying, though; holds space for the dying; renders them visible to themselves. Maybe some face their own death without fear. Did anyone do this for Simone Weil, I wonder? Maybe that's the point of everything.

May 2019, I finish the end-of-life doula training course.

November 2019, I complete training as a hospice volunteer.

March 2020, I sit with a dying patient in a nursing home; a state of emergency is called three days later.

Airborne disease. Respiratory illness. A global threat. Everything now in relationship.

✴✴✴

Despite all this relation-building you still feel that she is alien to you. You don't really get her, so you keep digging deeper and deeper and still nothing. From all the self-taught medieval art history you know that she's telling you, "Stop clinging to me," "you must let go of me," but you cannot stop. You keep reaching out your hands, and the clinging is so painful, and the letting go is so painful. You just want to know the answer, but you can no longer remember the question, or when you think of it, it is like a dream question that unravels in your hands.

You wonder if she is everything and every person you have ever loved. Is she the image of your complicated grief? You wonder if she is everything you feel is dying in yourself and in the world. Is she the image of your ambiguous loss?[8]

Right now, you are still making your way through this image. Still trying to connect your hands to hers, assuming that this is the image that answers the question, "what changes?" You will not really know until you are at the end, reassuring yourself. No character knows where they are in their own story when they are still in it. And when you get to the end, will this still be the obstacle you think it is as you move through it, or will the meaning change? You sense that this question is important, but you can't say why.

Typically, the image that crystallizes a change is something active. In a tragedy, for instance, it is knowledge helpfully delivered by a messenger. If Simone Weil is a messenger, she's like the annoying little boy in Samuel Beckett's *Waiting for Godot* (1954) who spends all that time traveling toward you only to tell you that there is no message, that you can continue to wait, but he won't remember who you are, and will deliver the same non-message to you the next day. You wait anyway. What the characters in *Godot* are really waiting for is recognition, which is exactly what Simone Weil is refusing you (see Fuchs 2007).

At some point you finally realize that this might be the point. She is not interested in your personality, she is not interested in your "I," and she is not interested in any of your unique connections to her. "There is something sacred in every man," writes Weil, "but it is not his person. Nor yet is it the human personality. It is this man; no more, and no less" (Weil 1986: 50). Later she writes, "everything that is impersonal in man is sacred, and nothing else" (Weil 1986: 54). You think your story is about going toward a coherent character, but Weil suggests that it is about nonidentification with your character.

Let's say you are an actor and your "personality" is your character. If Stanislavski is your director, he tells you to absorb yourself in that character *as if* it is your entire identity. But if Brecht is your director? You come at this relationship according to the alienation effect so that you, as actor, must act as a kind of a witness to this personality-character that you are performing. In between the actor-as-witness-consciousness and the personality-as-character, there is a gap. For Brecht, the distance between performer and the character means that the actor appears alien to the spectator; "alien to the point of arousing surprise." In this way, "everyday things are removed from the realm of the self-evident" (Brecht 1961: 131). You pay attention to this gap. You pay attention for years—remaining as receptive as is possible given your impatient nature. You are never sure if this gap is between you-as-witness and you-as-personality, or between you and Simone Weil, or if there are really any bookends at all. After a while you suspect that if you pay close-enough attention, everything is the gap.

"*Bardo* means gap," says Chogyam Trungpa, "it is not only a suspension after we die, but also a suspension in the living situation; death happens in the living situation as well" (2003: 2). In his commentary to *The Tibetan Book of the Dead*, Chogyam Trungpa explains that the focus on the dead person misses the point. He says that one could refer to this book as "The Tibetan Book of Birth," or better still, "The Tibetan Book of Space," as "space contains birth and death; space creates the environment in which to behave and act, it is the fundamental environment which provides the inspiration for *The Tibetan Book of the Dead*" (2003: 1).

This is a completely different concept of death, and you wonder about his ideas while reflecting on your obsession with Simone Weil's death. She is alone. There are seven mourners at her funeral. There are supposed to be eight people in attendance, but the priest never arrives. She is buried at No. 79 in Bybrook Cemetery in Ashford, Kent. Somewhere in all the noisy judgments people record about her life and her death, you listen into the gap. Catherine of Siena's name whispers itself in your ear—the patron saint of nurses, one of the world's first end-of-life doulas who shares remarkable similarities with Simone Weil, and inexplicably sends you to study her art. Catherine of Siena as a bardo-surfer, a companion into the unknown and unknowable space of our most personal impersonal human experience.

***

There is one other thing to which you pay careful attention when studying Weil: her hands. You wonder about her hands if for no other reason than the fact that they play a huge role in Hildegard of Bingen's story when God demands she write down everything she sees and hears, in the painted medieval images of the *Noli me tangere*, and, of course, in the story of Duse's beautiful and beautifully performing hands and the plaster casts made of them. In other words, you get interested simply because you want to see if this series of analogical correspondences between a mystic and her hands is also true for Simone Weil. It is a testing of a mathematical relationship—a geometric relationship—to which Weil would certainly approve. Weil's epistemologies are always grounded in mathematics: "Mathematics is the capacity rigorously to reason on the non-representable," she writes in one of her notebooks (qtd in Meltzer 2001: 615). How you come to know what you know, or, more likely for Weil, how you come to discover the truth, has its origins or foundation in a mathematical relationship.

What of Simone Weil's hands? You go searching for clues and find an essay by Francoise Meltzer (2001) entitled, "The Hands of Simone Weil." There is elegant design here, or, at least that's how you come to think of the fact that after your meticulous examination of her person, the most surprising thing that you find out about her is also the most impersonal: the hand is what makes you human, and therefore, for Weil, sacred. Yet, much like her writing, and her thinking, and her actions in the world, Weil's hands are a problem for her. Meltzer writes that "she could not make her hands useful or rapid—neither in factory work nor in writing" (2001: 623). Instead, for Weil, the hand is a *metaxu*—"both an obstacle and a way to truth" (2001: 624).

Metaxu (μεταξύ) is defined in Plato's *Symposium* as the "in-between" or "middle ground," and while the hand is "in-between" psyche and soma, thought and techne, invisible and visible for all of us, for Weil this *metaxu*, or bridge, is not easy crossing. She cannot take her hands for granted, and this fact alone might make her aware of some mystery, some gap between the invisible and visible worlds, where another kind of consciousness is possible. If her hands were not a problem for her, you wonder if she would still be Simone Weil. Like it or not, there is still something personal about our own hands even if most of us have them.

In honor of Simone Weil's hands—all that they accomplished and all that they made impossible—you end this lecture by performing a playlet with Pythagoras. One of Weil's favorite philosophers, he has his own way of apprehending how the mystery of the hand, its truth, has its origins in what is by turns referred to as the most irrational and the most beautiful number.

***

Palm pilot
Location: Mystery School in Mystery Land,
probably Greece, also probably Ancient

Pythagoras Why have you brought me into this?
You I was going to ask you the same thing.
Pythagoras This is your mystery, not mine.
You Is it though?

Pythagoras What do you mean?

You Tell me about the number five.

Pythagoras Why do you want to know? Who sent you here?

You Stop the drama, P, I think we both know who sent me.

Pythagoras We do?

You Sure we do.

Pythagoras Okay. What do you want to know?

You Why do I keep seeing so many hands? Everywhere I look, even when I close my eyes, they're waving at me—not whole people, just hands, five fingers and a palm.

Pythagoras You want to know who belongs to all these hands?

You Um, yeah, that would be brilliant, thanks.

Pythagoras (*laughs*)

You (*blank stare*)

Pythagoras You're so earnest!

You (*blank stare*)

Pythagoras You must realize that everyone has hands; they're not specific.

You So there's no meaning?

Pythagoras Everything has meaning.

You But what's the story?

Pythagoras What story?

You Exactly.

Pythagoras (*blank stare*)

You I can't tell if I'm getting lost in their story or they're lost in mine.

Pythagoras You mean, the hands?

You Uh, yes, please pay attention.

Pythagoras You're in the same story.

You How?

Pythagoras "How?" is a better question.

You Okay, *how* are we in the same story?

Pythagoras Because that is the nature of five: every part has the character of the whole.

You So I'm a fractal?

Pythagoras This isn't about you.

You (*blank stare*)

Pythagoras (*sighs; looks to his sundial for the time*) five fingers, five toes, five limbs of the human body, five regular solids, the perfect fifth in music, five points in a pentangle, which is the golden ratio, or golden mean, or the magical Phi. From either an arithmetic or geometrical point of view, the pentangle is a figure that keeps coming back to where it started, self-replicating, an endless knot.

You So my play is written from the point of view of a pentangle? That's weird.

Pythagoras Okay, you're a fractal, or what the medievals who invented your play might call a microcosm.

You ???

Pythagoras The golden ratio is in human physical proportions, music, shell spirals, pinecones, flower petals, seed heads, you get it?

You ???

Pythagoras It's used to build the Great Pyramid, the Parthenon…

You ???

Pythagoras The Milky Way galaxy, the shape of hurricanes, the diameter of Saturn to its rings?

You I sense you're a bit frustrated with something.

Pythagoras ALL IS NUMBER!

You Oh, that.

Pythagoras "Oh, that?!?!" *That* is everything!

You So is everything too much to ask? What it all means? How it's all connected?

Pythagoras I'm not a playwright, I'd need to ask Sophocles, but I'm fairly certain he'd say that it is asking way too much of your play.

You You mean my life?

Pythagoras (*a bit bored now*) What is it you really want to know?

You You mean, why am I here?

Pythagoras Okay, you can frame it that way, yes, why are you here?

You No, I mean, that's my actual question.

Pythagoras (*laughs*) That's not my business.
Black out.

Notes

1 Anthony Kubiak (1991) writes: "Whereas Aristotle sees this movement linearly in terms of *anagnoresis* (recognition), *peripeteia* (reversal), and *catastrophe* … the Church, in its sublimation of the theatrical to the historical in the enactment of the Mass, inverts the Aristotelian order, and posits the catastrophic event first (the Crucifixion), followed by the reversal (the Resurrection), ending with recognition (Christ's appearance to his followers)" (1991: 54).

2 Simone Weil (1909–1943) "philosophized on thresholds and across borders," and her "persistent desire for truth and justice led her to both elite academies and factory floors, political praxis and spiritual solitude. At different times she was an activist, a pacifist, a militant, a mystic, and an exile; but throughout, in her inquiry into reality and orientation to the good, she remained a philosopher" (see "Simone Weil,"< https://plato.stanford.edu/entries/simone-weil/> accessed June 19, 2023). Born in Paris to Jewish parents, Simone and her brother, André—himself a math prodigy, founder of the Bourbaki group, and a distinguished mathematician at the Princeton Institute for Advanced Studies—were raised agnostic among bourgeois French culture. Weil was a precocious student and by her teens had mastered Ancient Greek and several modern languages. She studied at the Lycée Fénelon (1920–4) and Lycée Victor Duruy, Paris (1924–5), graduating with baccalauréat. She

then continued her studies at the Lycée Henri IV (1925–8). In 1928, Weil finished first in the entrance examination for the École Normale Supérieure.

3   In Simone Weil's *Waiting for God* (2009)—a posthumous collection of essays and letters, compiled by Father J. M. Perrin and Gustave Thibon, and comprising Weil's spiritual autobiography—I came across a letter she wrote to Father Perrin, a Dominican priest she had befriended when her family was forced to move to Marseilles in October 1940 to escape Nazi persecution. Father Perrin served as a kind of spiritual director and spiritual friend to Weil. While Weil was Jewish by birth, and became enamored with Christianity in her twenties, she never converted to any religious faith in the orthodox sense, wanting to live at the "intersection of Christianity and everything that is not Christianity" (2009: 32). In a letter written just days before her departure in May 1942, she prefaces her account of her experience in Assisi by writing that, in adolescence, she "saw the problem of God as a problem of data of which could not be obtained here below." She continues: "I decided that the only way of being sure not to reach the wrong solution, which seemed to me the greatest possible evil, was to leave it alone. So I left it alone. I neither affirmed or denied anything ... I thought that, being in this world, our business was to adopt the best attitude with regard to the problems of this world, and that such an attitude did not depend upon the solution of the problem of God" (2009: 22). This changed in Assisi in 1937. She tells Perrin that this is where she had her first mystical experience. "There, alone in the little twelfth-century Romanesque chapel [inside] Santa Maria degli Angeli, an incomparable marvel of purity where Saint Francis often used to pray something stronger than I was compelled me for the first time in my life to go down on my knees" (2009: 26).

4   Robert Coles, MD, professor of psychiatry and medical humanities at Harvard, and one of Simone Weil's biographers (2001) explains that there is little evidence to suggest that she had anorexia nervosa, a condition "characterized by extreme weight loss, body-image disturbances and an intense fear of becoming obese" (2001: 27). Anna Freud, renowned psychologist and a contemporary of Weil, similarly states that "Simone Weil doesn't seem to have had any delusions of

obesity, or at least, hasn't described her *fatness* as the enemy" (emphasis in the original; qtd in Coles 2001: 27). Freud compassionately suggests that instead of "call[ing] her anything clinical, we should instead try to see the world as she did and try to understand what she felt and said, and why" (2001: 28).

5   For the four months Weil lived in London before her death, she wrote prodigiously for the *Free French*. She slept only three hours a night and spent the rest of the time working on reports, including one that would be published after her death as *The Need for Roots* (1952b).

6   It took 200 years for the population levels in the world to reach its pre-1347 rate. Beginning when Catherine was just six years old, she had a vision of Christ that established not only her vow to Jesus as a bridegroom, but also her fierce asceticism. Suzanne Noffke remarks that as she "grew into adolescence her determination never to marry kept pace with a regimen of fasting and physical discipline which increased in intensity until she became incapable of eating normally" (2012: xix). In addition to her fasting, Catherine, like Simone Weil, did everything she could to make herself unattractive to the opposite sex so that she would not be forced to marry. After much cajoling of her parents, they gave up their fight for her to marry and allowed her to become a member of the lay Third Order of Saint Dominic (coincidentally, the same order as Simone Weil's spiritual advisor).

7   Raymond of Capua, Catherine of Siena's confessor and friend, writes in his *Legenda*, "everyone has something to say against this holy virgin." Her contemporaries found her habits difficult to understand. "She drank only a little cold water and chewed on bitter herbs while spitting out the substance," according to Raymond. Her only nourishment was from the host alone. Catherine explains: "When I cannot receive the Sacrament, it satisfies me to be nearby and to see it; indeed, even to see a priest who has touched the Sacrament consoles me greatly, so that I lose all memory of food" (qtd in Bell 1985: 26). The pointing out of the relationship between seeing and eating shares striking resonance with Simone Weil's statement that "Man's great affliction, which begins with infancy and accompanies him till death, is that looking and eating are two different operations. Eternal beatitude is the state where to look is to eat" (*GG* 1952a: 100). For both women, food was a complicated matter. For a

reading that places Weil in a relational context with a different set of mystics, see Carson (2005).

8 According to Pauline Boss (2000), there are

> two basic kinds of ambiguous loss. In the first type, people are perceived by family members as *physically absent* but psychologically present, because it is unclear whether they are dead or alive. Missing soldiers and kidnapped children illustrate this type of loss in its catastrophic form. ... In the second type of ambiguous loss, a person is perceived as physically present but *psychologically absent*. This condition is illustrated in the extreme by people with Alzheimer's disease, addictions, and other chronic mental illnesses. ... In more everyday situations, people who are excessively preoccupied with their work or other outside interests also fit this category. ... The inability to resolve such ambiguous loss is due to the *outside* situation, not to internal personality defects. (emphases in the original; 2000: 8–10)

Boss's theory of ambiguous loss reemerged during the Covid-19 pandemic as a means of finding language for the way that people experienced loss without being quite sure what it is they had lost yet. "Unlike death, an ambiguous loss may never allow people to achieve the detachment that is necessary for normal closure. ... People can't start grieving because the situation is indeterminate. It feels like a loss, but it is not *really* one. The confusion freezes the grieving process" (emphasis in the original; 2000: 10–11).

Lecture 5

On Acting and Not Acting

Actors in a mystery play are always aware that they are both actor and character. They never forget that they are double. Who cares? Why is this important? Let's pretend we're in York, England. It is around 1465. Why? Because you know from historical research that it is around this time that the city officials began keeping a record of the mystery plays.[1]

Mystery plays are performed in a cycle on one very long day. Spectators watch the enactment of biblical stories, around forty-eight, from Creation to The Last Judgment. Each one is placed on a wagon that serves as the stage space, and the wagons move through the streets as actors perform their scene over and over, performing plays simultaneously throughout the city.

At any one time, as many as ten or more actors could be performing Jesus. Now, there are many reasons for this, but your point is to emphasize that there is never any attempt to pretend that you're enacting a psychological character. There is no *one* actor who is personally identified with Jesus. Actors aren't standing around asking themselves, "what's my motivation?" and then pulling from their own lives to fill in the gaps. You're standing in for the Son of God, not pretending to be him. Medieval people know that this is a ludicrous idea, not to mention that in their world, it is also sacrilegious (see Aronson-Lehavi 2011).

Never forget that the doubleness is always there. You're always pointing to yourself, saying something like, *I'm an actor and this is a character*. You're always pointing to another reality, but you don't confuse your reality with the one you perform. They exist simultaneously. This is true whether you're acting the role of a deity or not. You're still pointing, still making everything double.

Take, for instance, the trade guilds that produce these lavish spectacles. Do you know what trade guilds are called in Middle English? A mystery. Yes, a theatrical play on words that means both a divine revelation, or spiritual truth, and a trade or craft. Anyway, the important thing is that in this town at this time, trade guilds, wanting to demonstrate their proficiency in their craft, sponsor and perform a play to highlight their talents. Not their acting talents, but their talents as tradesmen. This means that the shipwrights build and perform the story of *Noah's Ark*, the bakers prepare and perform the story of the *Last Supper*, and so on (see Justice 1979).

Now, the one that you want to discuss, the one that really gets to the heart of the matter, is *The Crucifixion*. Do you know who performs this one? The pinners, the makers of pins and nails. The members of this guild, who make nails, play the role of Jesus's crucifiers, those who nail him to the cross. This doubleness is so interesting to you. It is not simply that the past is made present on stage in this strange way, that Jerusalem is now England with a Yorkshire accent, but that the present also changes the past. Yes?

Perhaps you watch, or, more likely today, read this play and think to yourself that maybe the people who nailed Jesus to the cross are picked simply because they are the ones with the nails—not that they are more hateful, or malicious, it's just that on that day their profession is not on their side. The same tools that yesterday built Martha a shelter are today used to crucify a man that many believe to be God, or the Son of God at any rate.

You don't know this to be true. For all you know maybe they feel proud to be murderers, but you suspect that the medieval playwright and the medieval actors and the medieval trade guilds got something right. Picked up on the human absurdity of it all. These performers aren't trying to figure out the psychological motivation of the crucifiers. No. They learn that by simply following their physical behavior, their actions ... listen, you and I both know it doesn't take psychological identification to find yourself enacting a character who is long gone. You simply need to step into their mold, move like they do for a while, feel their patterns in your muscles, in your bones. Then, in some inexplicable way, they show up, some of their energy is now part of your energy system.

Think of it as a bit like performing a dead relative. This relative appears to you after a particularly good performance and congratulates you for understanding his patterns so well. In fact, the dead relative remarks that it is as if the patterns you are performing are yours and not his. The relative, knowing he is an asshole, then says that he is grateful that you are only performing the pattern for demonstration purposes.

But maybe it comes as a surprise when this ancestor from the past starts talking to you about patterns. Maybe you aren't aware that you restored a particular pattern of behavior through your actions. Maybe you *do* think it is your own behavior. Maybe this is because this pattern lay dormant for 1,000 years. Let's say that an ancient historian writing a chronicle of one of the men who crucified Jesus records that *these actions are now buried with Crucifier #1 and will not be carried into the future.* But our dear historian friend forgets, or does not want to remember, that Crucifer #1 has children and that something of his pattern will be imprinted in those children and his children's children. Maybe, as in the case with evil and traumatic actions, the pattern is repressed. Maybe it skips generations until much later your own kid is on a pageant wagon in York nailing a fake Jesus to a cross and wondering why he's finding it so satisfying and scary, why he can't stop his hammer, why he wants to perform this again and again, and why he can't understand his compulsion to repeat.

You stop and look around the classroom. You see me laughing and you smile. You understand, before I do, that at some time in the future you will be narrating this for a different reason, in a different context. You become aware at this precise moment that the past and present are simultaneous for you, and that time is something you are always devising and revising. You simply look at me, and recognize that you enjoy playing with the dead, that play and death are second nature to you, and you cannot understand one without the other. For now, the universe has provided you with the only space available for you to do this work, work that will lead you further and further from the stage.

You call on me while I'm laughing. You're still smiling. You say, "you, back there, what can you tell me about Jesus and the actor who's playing Jesus in this crucifixion?" You see me stop laughing. You wonder to yourself if I know about the roles the two of us will perform in the future. I answer you, hesitantly, "they're both in a lot of pain?" Yes, you say, yes they are.

***

Our smiling friend in the back makes a very good point, you say. Both Jesus and the actor playing Jesus are in a lot of pain. Jesus's pain is understood, but the actor's? Why is he in pain? Let's be clear here: the actor is not in pretend pain. He's on that cart going through York all day long. All day long he's being stretched over a wooden cross, and while he isn't nailed to the cross (but you can tell stories of where this has happened, and more recently), he is manhandled, strapped with ropes, and then made to hang on the cross for long durations of time. As you can imagine, this is crazy painful. So what does this tell us about his pain?

There is pain in both realities—it's not just the character's pain, but the actor's pain too. As any good performance artist will tell you, this is a really *authentic* performance. It's not merely theatre. There's no faking it. Performance artists love this kind of pain, love to cut themselves, and flog themselves, or throw themselves down staircases, or shoot themselves. They love it because it is so real. They get very attached to their pain. They get so attached that they often forget what the medieval actor always knows: that it is not just their pain. The medieval actor says, *yes, this pain is mine, but it didn't start with me; my pain is pointing somewhere else.* The medieval actor knows that you must *feel* this pain with your own hands to know how to point it in a different direction.

If you're a medieval actor, then it is very easy to know with whom the pain originates: *I am an actor playing Jesus, and while my pain is crazy real, and I can't wait to get off this f-ing wagon, this pain didn't start with my performance. Or it did start with my performance, but once my performance of this pain stops, so does the pain itself.* The medieval actor does not carry it off the stage because he knows that his pain is not personal, even though he feels it.

Here's the paradox: depending on how you reenact this performance, one of two things can happen: you can be freed from the suffering you carry, which means your pain can give birth to a whole new consciousness. Or, you can get stuck in a Crucifixion complex, where you are always being tortured, are always the victim. This is serious because one leads to liberation and the other can lead to death, often by suicide, you add distractedly.

Okay. You're definitely not talking about acting.

Let's say once upon time you have a friend who is a really great performance artist. And this performance artist likes to reenact medieval religious rituals but doesn't call them medieval religious rituals. He has this famous performance meant for only one audience member at a time. It's called *Foot Washing for the Sole*.[2]

He washes people's feet at festivals all over the world. It is really popular. People love it and talk about it as immersive performance, one-to-one performance, solo performance, *very avant-garde stuff*, that's how it is discussed. Funny that no one says, oh, he's enacting Jesus washing his disciples' feet at the Last Supper. People love a good religious ritual so long as it is framed as art, and you don't have to talk about its origins. Also, there is no theatrical context for his performance. This is just *authentic* performance art. It is just about the performer doing this series of gestures of washing feet repeatedly, sometimes for many hours at a time, for multiple days. He's a durational performer, an endurance artist. But honestly, isn't Jesus this too?

Hypothetically speaking, let's pretend your friend is performing this as a medieval mystery play: if this is a mystery play, it would be on a wagon right around the scene of the Last Supper, you say, which is when Jesus washes the feet of his disciples. This means that it is probably sponsored by the baker's guild, you add distractedly.

Your point is that at this moment in the story, Jesus knows he's going to die. So, he washes their feet and tells them to go and do as he has done. He sets an example of how to carry love forward, how to be of service to others. "A humanitarian challenge," your friend says in an interview with the British Council. He is quoting the bible and talking about *Foot Washing for the Sole* when he says this.[3]

When your friend, the performance artist, is in this performance, and other people are bearing witness, he is in the midst of carrying love forward. He is a living gesture of this love that is carried body to body, teacher to student. Every time a body carries this love forward, it takes a different form, and his form is performance art, but the love defies all genres.

Now, if you, personally, had this Last Supper context for his performance at the time that he is performing this piece in which you, yourself, participate, then maybe you would know what is going to happen next. But you don't have this context and neither does your friend, the performance artist. He just thinks that this washing of feet will go on indefinitely. But all performances must come to an end; you must move on to the next act at some point.

If you know you are at the Last Supper, you say again, if you know what he's preparing, maybe you can prepare yourself too. Sure, Jesus's next act is the Crucifixion. But your friend, the performance artist, forgets that he is in a performance. Because he is not a medieval actor, he doesn't remember that his performance is not about him, it is not personal.

A Crucifixion complex is not something that happens on the stage or in the performance space, you say, but something that happens in your head. It is not a problem of medieval psychology because medieval psychology never confuses the action of performing pain and psychological identification with pain, the origin of which is never Jesus. If you want to know the origin of the patterns that will destroy you, shake the family tree. After all, it is Jesus's father who tells him he must die.

For psychological complexes there is no audience bearing witness, so you can easily forget that you are not alone. Also, you can forget that Jesus didn't take his own life—he is condemned to death. But everyone loves you!

Apologies. You are beginning to see double.

"Where are you right now?" That's the question you keep asking your friend, the performance artist, when you write to him in your journal: "Do you know where you are yet?" And also, "Why did you have to kill yourself?"

Your friend's death remains a mystery to you, and you are reminded of the double meaning of the medieval word mystery. The definition of mystery is so much bigger than what you do, your trade, but what you do *will* take you there. So, you make some lecture notes on another performance artist who seems obsessed with her own death.

***

The Deaths of Marina Abramović: Lecture Notes

Marina Abramović (1946–) is a placeholder for me. That's what I think reading *Walk through Walls* (2016), her memoire. It's a weird thought. The self-proclaimed "grandmother" of performance art has many groupies. I'm not one of them. Later, I think she might be my actual grandmother. Not *actual* actual. Vague family resemblance.

Performance artists and theatre artists obey different rules regarding story. Theatre is interested in things like plot. Performance art wants to strip back theatre's "fakery," and show the blueprint of story.

"Performance artists always work with the materials from their own lives," Abramović says. This is why it is often so boring.

If you're Abramović, you sit a long time, repeat gestures over hours, or days, or months, cut yourself, let others cut you, repeatedly bump into a naked person, walk halfway across the Great Wall of China to break up with that formerly naked person, meditate until you pass out, heal people with crystals, direct a choir of Tibetan monks. You know, *real* shit.[4]

The only two times I see her perform, she is not doing real shit. It interests me. I never believe performers are just performing themselves. Theatre's fakery is always the *real* real. Theatre never forgets about the ghosts. But I would say that.

The first time I see her is in 2011. I convince my colleagues that we should all take the train from Glasgow to Manchester, England, to attend Robert Wilson's *The Life and Death of Marina Abramović* (2011).[5] It is so beautiful, and she is so bad that it's kind of great. She plays her mother, too. Her mother is an abusive monster. Top member in the communist party in Belgrade. Her father a mere shadow. Unfaithful. Also scarred by war. She tells the story of her abusive mother *repeatedly*: in interviews, performances, her memoire. Everywhere.

I think about her compulsion to repeat as a blueprint while reading Mark Wolynn's *It Didn't Start with You: How Inherited Family Trauma Shapes Who We Are and How to End the Cycle* (2016). Shake the family tree, he says.

If we are in her childhood, are we also in her mother's pain, her father's disconnection, all three? And if we are, are we also in her mother's childhood, her grandmother's pain, her grandfather's disconnection? Or are we in her father's childhood, his mother's disconnection, his father's pain? Our stories are never that original.

The second time I see her perform, it is an accident. But is it, really? For one week only, the week I am in London to research her early work at the Live Art Development agency, the Serpentine Gallery is producing Abramović's *The Life* (2019)—the latest iteration in a number of her performances about death. I find out about it the day before my flight.

"The first large-scale performance exhibit using Mixed Reality anywhere in the world."[6] I get fitted with a "Magic Leap One lightweight wearable spatial computing device." I am guided into the main gallery space where I am told to stare at a diagram on the wall just inside the entrance. I "calibrate" my glasses so that Abramović and I can be on the same frequency for the duration of the 19-minute performance.

I'm taken to the edge of a roped off 5-meter circle at the center of the gallery floor. From a body of blue light, she appears in a red dress in the middle of the circle looking every bit like the Serbian performance artist version of a Princess Leia hologram.

Standing at the edge of this circle with total strangers reminds me of the time I stand in a circle with strangers at the Omega Institute in New York. Mark Wolynn is facilitating something impossible to categorize. A *New Yorker* writer once described family constellation therapy as part theatre, part therapy, and part séance.[7] Whatever it is, this man does not forget that the present is also a history of restless ghosts.

There are so many people in this family constellation circle whose origins are in Eastern Europe.

Stories of dead ancestors in pogroms, war camps, of family abuse, of hunger. So many ghosts, my mind is reeling.

We are asked to stand in as representatives for other people's dead relatives—not to act them out, but as placeholders, fleshy holograms, for the absent ancestors: sharecroppers, holocaust victims, women in matriarchal lineages, siblings, black sheep, the invisible and unnamed, everyone. As participants intuitively find their way to various locations in the circle based on the details of someone's story, it is clear what James Hillman, archetypal psychologist, meant when he said that events don't tell a story, they reveal a pattern.

People think of family legacies in material terms, but ancestors' legacies to their offspring is more often than not, the legacy of their unfinished business—the patterns they are either incapable or unable to break. For the living, this often takes the form of repeating these patterns in a play we'll call "unconscious loyalty." One epigeneticist refers to this phenomenon of inherited trauma as ancestral ghosts in your genome.[8]

Back in the Serpentine Gallery, I stand motionless for a long time on the edge of the roped-off circle where my white-lab-coat-wearing helper places me when entering the gallery. He tells me I can stay there, or if I want to walk around the circle to do so in a clockwise fashion. Since I wrongly assume that my point of view will remain the same regardless of where I stand, I stay. After about 10 minutes, I get restless and start walking. As I do, I see that Abramović is moving too—she is walking around that circle as a three-dimensional hologram. Of course, this is what augmented reality/mixed reality means, but having never experienced it, I default to thinking of the image as virtual reality. It *does* matter where I stand. This wordless, plotless performance is still a fully relational experience.

Walking slowly in circles as I watch her move in relation to my own movements, it slowly dawns on me why I have the vague feeling that she's a placeholder: my great grandmother has two daughters, my grandmother has two daughters, my mother has two daughters, and my sister has two daughters. Do we always give birth to our ancestors' pain? How much unconscious loyalty do we repeat in our life patterns?

I continue walking and wonder, not for the first time, if we heal our ancestors by not repeating them.

***

What stays after you're gone? You think that patterns remain. To the degree that you see them or repeat them you suppose you can think of them as a hologram, but that is not your preference. Even still, without the performance artist's hologram, you can't say for sure that you would ever see this pattern of your ancestors coming in two by two, or three by three, a mother and two daughters. At first you think the answer is clear, that if you just ensure that you don't repeat your ancestors, all will be well. And, of course, you take this literally, so you don't have children.

But the performance artist does not have a child who she abuses, and locks in a closet, and hits in the face, or to whom she does a bunch of other horrid stuff. She doesn't have to reproduce children to reproduce her mother's patterns. In many of her performances she almost dies by her own hand. And maybe it is not a surprise that she speaks of her mother constantly, even plays her in *The Life and Death of Marina Abramović* (2011). Her mother's energy is always there fueling her pain, her disconnection. And yet, here she is, both virtual and fully connected, alive in another way, a way that doesn't deny the mother, but doesn't repeat her either. What changes for the performance artist? How does she find a way to redirect this pain? What image does she pass through in her own drama so that the pain that could destroy her starts to liberate her?

Picture this, you say: you're a soon-to-be-famous performance artist. You're Yugoslavian, and you're in Edinburgh, Scotland, and it's 1973. You're about to perform at Melville College, a pop-up venue for the Edinburgh Fringe Festival. You're preparing for your first performance. Up until this point, you work on sound installations, but you haven't yet used your body in your artwork. Not until today.

You're intense, and so is this performance. You feel like you're going to get sick before you perform, you're terrified, you can hardly breathe. At this point, your art is a matter of life and death. That's what you recall in your memoire many years later when you are a famous performance artist (see Abramović 2016: 58–61). And while you know this is true, even if it is melodramatic, do you ever really know how true it is? Because if this performance is about anything, it is about life and death. Yours, yes, but not just yours.

This is how you describe this first performance of yours in the retrospective of your early work.

Rhythm 10 (1973): Preparation

I lay a sheet of white paper on the floor. I lay ten knives of different shapes and sizes on the floor. I place two cassette recorders with microphones on the floor.

Performance

I switch on the first cassette recorder. I take the knife and plunge it, as fast as I can, into the flesh between the outstretched fingers of my left hand. After each cut, I change to a different knife. Once all the knives (all the rhythms) have been used, I rewind the tape. I listen to the recording of the first performance. I concentrate. I repeat the first part of the performance. I pick up the knives in the same sequence, adhere to the same rhythm and cut myself in the same places. In this performance, the mistakes of the past and those of the present are synchronous. I rewind the same tape and listen to the dual rhythm of the knives. I leave.

—Marina Abramović; instructions from the *Rhythm 10* performance.[9]

It is certainly not your most dangerous performance, as there are several that put your life at great risk.[10] And though you are emphatic that you're not interested in dying, or death, you highly doubt the latter. You want to push through and past the pain, the physical, yes, but also the psychological, the emotional, and fear, too. You are successful at this. In fact, you don't know of another artist who is as successful at pushing past the limits of the body in quite the way that you do. But this is not the reason for bringing this performance to your attention. Aside from the fact that the performance is played entirely on your own hands, which, you must admit, is rather intriguing given the shape of your own mystery, there are other reasons that you are drawn to this particular play of the hands.

You're interested in repetition. One hand stabbing the space between the other hand with those knives (see Figure 5.1). Ten knives, ten fingers, ten rhythms. You say that the repetition of the same thing over and over generates enormous power. You say that this is why ancient cultures base their ritual structures on repetition. This is interesting because it is true, but also tricky. Doing the same thing over and over is often considered a form of insanity, but you suppose that it's just insanity if you expect different results. What you're really getting at here is that repetition is not only an important part of ritual, but it is also a key component to traumatic experience.

The harrowing actions in your performance art remind you of Freud's theory of trauma and the repetition compulsion (see Freud 1914). Phenomenologically speaking, trauma always happens in the present. Trauma is not a memory but an experience that is happening in the now. The "origin" story of trauma is traumatic experience itself. It does not operate like a play with a beginning, middle, and end. Your inability to slow it down, stop it, and witness it *as you are experiencing it* means that it operates more like a sound loop than an image. But what if you *can* witness it as you are experiencing it? What happens then?

The cassette recorder records the sound of knives plunging between your fingers. You cut yourself, so you pick up the next knife,

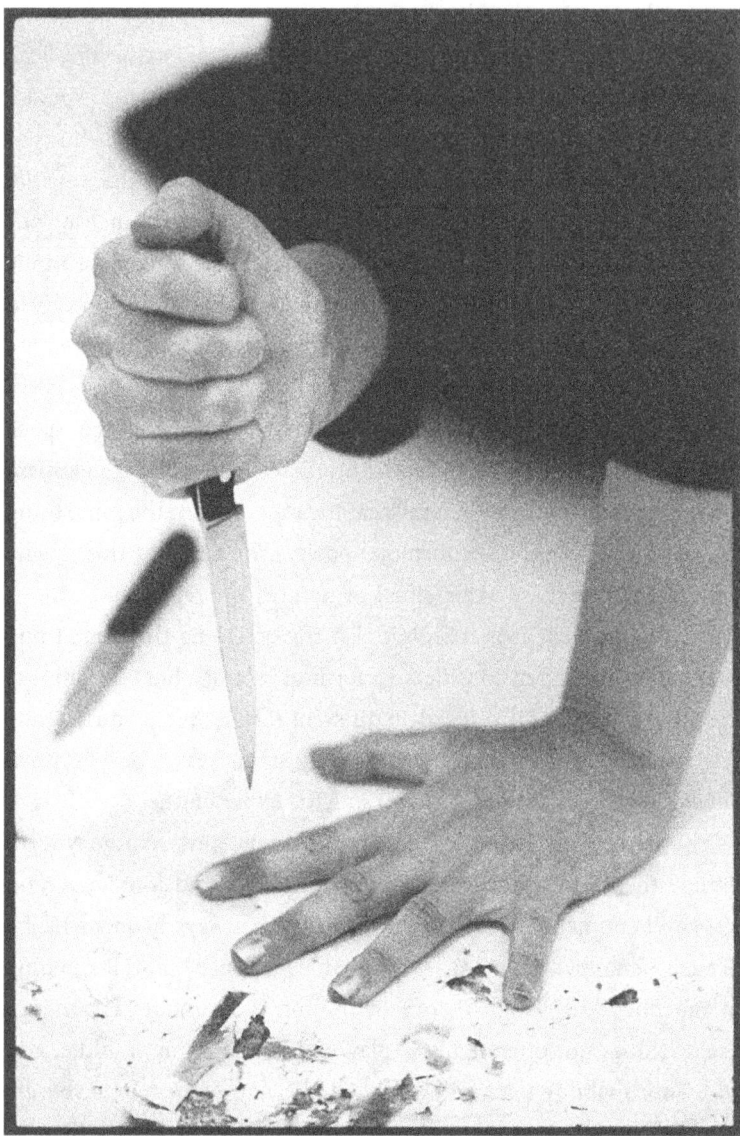

Figure 5.1. Marina Abramović, *Rhythm 10*, Performance, 1 Hour, Museo d'Arte Contemporanea Villa Borghese, Rome, Italy, 1973. © Marina Abramović, Courtesy of the Marina Abramović Archives.

and start again. You do this over and over until you use all ten knives. You stop the tape. Rewind. Listen. Then you play the rhythms on the tape and match them to the rhythm of the knives that you plunge, again and again, in and through your hands. This is all recorded on a second recorder. After you use all ten knives again, you stop the second recorder, rewind the tape, and listen. *The mistakes of the past and those of the present are synchronous*, you say.

What are you really listening to when you listen to that tape? That's your big question. You wonder what mistakes you might be hearing, or, if in listening to the mistakes you start to hear something else? With the right hand holding the knife, you perform ritual repetition, while your left hand receives repeated traumatic cuts in present tense. On the one hand, the right, this power causes suffering, but you wonder if the other hand, the left, leads to your liberation.

It's interesting, too, because it is not a *story*, but just some sounds, or, more specifically, just some rhythms, even if they are rhythms that are also erratic and ill-advised. Is your mother attached to your story of trauma? Is she part of the rhythm of your past? What else are you playing with here? Is this personal? Sure, you're doing it to yourself and on your own hands, but maybe it is personal like the medieval actor who plays Jesus in York, or maybe it is personal like the medieval actor who plays Crucifier #1 in York because, in your case, your hands are each playing a different character, one the destroyer, one the redeemer. But, of course, they are just sounds, rhythms, and not characters, not part of a play, because what you do is real and not pretend.

Not a play, but still not solo, two hands, plus there is that transfixed audience. Can you make an audience a witness to your trauma? You must be able to do this since you do it. And since it is not framed as trauma, but performance art, there is an enormous energy that is created, an energy that might bring something else into that space because it is no longer simply real life, even though, of course, it is also real life.

But whatever it is that you are doing, whatever it is that you are listening to when you listen to the knives and the cuts, whatever is happening here, is not just happening to you. What you mean is that the synchronous sounds of the past and present are the sounds of your repeated trauma, but is it just yours? You wonder if your double past is full of your ancestors whose hands look like yours and who suffer at other people's hands, or, even more likely, suffer by their own hands. Maybe they are your mother's hands after all. Maybe you're here to redeem them. Is this why you listen closely, and then leave? Do the rhythms tell you to go? Do they tell you to stop repeating because you now, finally, really listen, and more importantly, now finally, really hear the rhythm to which you are listening? And maybe you hear this somehow because there is an audience?

The thing that you, yourself, still find mysterious, or sublime because it is enormously grand in this really quiet way, is that before this moment, you don't even understand that you are a performance artist. That just moments before this you think you will stop breathing with fear, you think you might actually die, you feel this to be true while you're setting up your white paper, and your cassette recorders, and your knives, feel this when the audience enters and sits around you. And then you start, and you notice the audience noticing your actions. Some in the audience are now famous (and now dead) performance artists, and you feel their energy, which is not yours, and you take it, and do something magical with it, and then give it back to them, so that you and the audience are both in another place and time for a while, which is to say, you are all entirely, miraculously, present. Which is to say that you play with death in such a way that you pass right through it without death even noticing that you're alive in another way. Can you hear it now?

In your memoir, you say that when you step into the performance space "*it's not you anymore.* You say it is not the you that you know" (Abramović 2016: 60; emphasis in the original). You say it is something else. You say that on the gymnasium floor of Melville College in Edinburgh, you become a receiver and transmitter of "Tesla-like energy" (2016: 60). You say the fear is gone and the pain is gone, and you become a person whom you don't know yet. Maybe art asks you to be curious about the Other who's already present. Maybe *you* are the mystery you seek.

Notes

The title of this lecture is taken from Michael Kirby (1972), "On Acting and Not-Acting," *TDR: The Drama Review* 16(1): 3–15. In the first paragraph, he sets out some of the parameters that speak to the issues of this lecture. He writes: "Acting means to feign, to simulate, to represent, to impersonate. As Happenings demonstrated, not all performing is acting. Although acting was sometimes used, the performers in Happenings generally tended to 'be' nobody or nothing other than themselves; nor did they represent, or pretend to be in, a time or place different than that of the spectator. They walked, ran, said words, sang, washed dishes, swept, operated machines and stage devices, and so forth, but they did not feign or impersonate" (1972: 3).

1 The entire series of 48–50 plays is known as the Corpus Christi play, or Corpus Christi cycle. Between 1463 and 1477, the city of York started keeping an official record of the play cycle. This *Register*, as it is known, is the sole surviving manuscript of the cycle of plays.
2 To read more about this performance, see Gough (2016).
3 To watch a recording of the interview with the British Council, see Howells (2011).
4 For a historical overview of Abramović's performance art, see Danto et al. (2010).
5 *The Life and Death of Marina Abramović* (2011), directed by Robert Wilson, begins and ends at her funeral. Three coffins appear on stage. This is a biographical detail. In Abramović's last will and testament, she requests that a series of actions be carried out in the event of her death:

> In case of my death I would like to have this following memorial ceremony:
>
> Three coffins.
>
> The first coffin with my real body.
>
> The second coffin with an imitation of my body.
>
> The third coffin with an imitation of my body.
>
> I would like to appoint that three persons would take care of the distribution of the three coffins in three different places in the world (America, Europe and Asia). The special instructions will be written and put in a sealed envelope, with their names and instructions to follow. …
>
> The ceremony should be a celebration of life and death combined. After the ceremony there will be a feast with a large cake made out of marzipan in the shape and looks of my body. I want the cake to be distributed to the present people. (Qtd in Westcott 2010: xiii)

6 To read more about Abramović's (2019) *The Life* at the Serpentine Gallery, see <https://www.serpentinegalleries.org/whats-on/marina-abramovic-life/ > accessed February 3, 2023.

7 See Bilger (2016).

8 See Skinner (2015).

9 See Media Art Net for description: <http://www.medienkunstnetz.de/works/rhythm-10-2/ > accessed February 3, 2023.

10 In Abramović's earliest work, a series of five performances called "Rhythms" (1973–4), Abramović tested the mental and physical limits of her own body. In *Rhythm 5* (1973), she lay in the middle of a large five-pointed star that she set on fire without realizing that fire removes oxygen from the air. Audience members pulled her out from inside the burning star when her leg caught fire, and she did not move because she had passed out from lack of oxygen. She then wondered how in future work she could use her body—conscious or not—without disrupting the performance. In *Rhythm 4* (1974), she placed her naked body in front of a powerful industrial fan directed at her open mouth. Audience members, watching from another room, did not realize she had passed

out. The performance continued. In *Rhythm 2* (1974), she took two drugs, one given for the treatment of extreme catatonia and the other for the treatment of extreme aggression. Finally, in *Rhythm 0*, her most infamous performance, seventy-two objects were placed on a table in a Naples art gallery and audience members were encouraged to use them on her in any way they like. She remains a passive object for a six-hour duration. For the first half of the performance the audience remained relatively benign. She was moved into a series of poses, written on with lipstick, and had her clothes ripped. During the second half of the performance, however, things took a drastic turn. "One person cut her neck with a razor blade then drank her blood. Another wove a thorn-covered rose around her neck. Finally, when an audience member placed a loaded pistol in Abramović's hand, and pointed it at her chest, the performance was stopped." To view images from the performances and to read more about the series, see <https://blogs.uoregon.edu/marinaabramovic/category/rhythm-series/> accessed February 3, 2023.

Lecture 6

The Theatre and Its Double

If you are the mystery you seek, does it change the direction and orientation of your life? Does this new direction help you to find yourself? Does this mean you are lost? And if you are (lost), and you do manage to locate yourself, do you immediately know it is *you*, or do you think it is someone else?

It is the *someone* part that is the trouble. Character: that old chestnut.

But the performance artist found her other self by listening and playing with sound and rhythm on her hands. She heard a pattern of something other who she later calls a person, but this person is a pattern first. And when it is a pattern and not herself, you suspect that there are many people involved. Many *dead* people. *Her* dead people. You like to think that as she plunges those knives through her fingers with her own hands, that her past, even the past that precedes her appearance on the planet, joins her in that space, that her repetition calls it forth: the worst patriarchs in the family and the worst parts of the war and the communist system that ruled their lives, even some spectral aspect of her abusive mother and all of the ways that abuse is carried forward. All of it. Here on the gymnasium floor. But this time, they are not here to see something repeat. They're here to see her bring it to an end. They're here to see the end of time. They're here to witness a change in time signature. You see this, you suspect, because you want this to be true of *your* dead ancestors.

In Resmaa Menakem's *My Grandmother's Hands: Racialized Trauma and the Pathways to Mending Our Hearts and Bodies* (2017), he begins by discussing his memory of his grandmother's stout hands that were formed into their shape by her labor of picking cotton from the age of four years old. Cotton plants have burrs that rip up the hands so that they are torn and bloody. Over time the skin becomes thicker and thicker so that they no longer bleed from the trauma of the labor. He ends this brief account of his grandmother's hands by telling the reader that even though she has died, "I can still feel her warm thick hands in mine" (2017: 4).

You remember hearing the story told by Patricia Williams in *The Alchemy of Race and Rights* (1992) of her attempt to trace a path to find her great-great grandmother, who was a slave, through her "great-great grandmother's owner and the father of her children," who, like Williams herself, was a lawyer (Gordon 1997: 5). Williams writes that she "sees her [great-great grandmother's] shape and his hand in the vast networking of our society, and in the evils and oversights that plague our lives and laws." Williams knows that she is not separate from her ancestors. "The force he [her great-great grandfather] was in her life, is the shape of my life today," she writes (Williams 1992: 19).

The trauma that Williams's great-great grandmother experienced because of "white-body supremacy," to use a phrase from Menakem (2017: xiii), is not at all the trauma that your ancestors experience who live inside the white bodies she references. In Menakem's hands, however, he initiates a practice that can help white-identified and Black-identified bodies heal together from the ongoing legacy of how white-bodied supremacy keeps us from relating—to ourselves, to each other, to a shared past, and to the world.

In his book, Menakem spends time reviewing the invention of whiteness.[1] While this hydra-headed history is long, winding, and of multiple origins, what you are most surprised to read about is Menakem's take on medieval trauma. For thousands of years before Europeans came to America, he writes, "human beings murdered, butchered, tortured, oppressed, abused, conquered, enslaved, and colonized one another" (2017: 59). Citing historians of medieval England, he tells us that for much of the Middle Ages, torture "was a spectator sport" (2017: 59). He suggests that the torture white Europeans meted out to each other was transferred to nonwhite bodies in the Americas when they start arriving in 1619—a kind of trauma response. You think about torture as a spectator sport and remember those postcards of lynching in the South that circulate like souvenirs in the 1890s—the same postcards that Ida B. Wells uses to launch her anti-lynching campaign over in England at the fin de siècle, and you think of the long, winding medieval tail of this history (see Gough 2014: 60-9).

You're reading Menakem's book and thinking of how your father's family—through one William Gough—arrives in St. Mary's County, Maryland, in the late 1650s from around the Isle of Wight—an island in England—though it is unclear if they are English? Welsh? Scottish? Irish? Maybe by way of some Dutch? What is known is that they are Catholic, and they hop on that ship that takes them to Maryland to escape religious persecution. As soon as they land in this state, they enter a system of governance where humans are turned into slaves and where other humans are systematically erased: the two fates that they are presumably trying to flee. One does not explain the other. But this idea of traumatic repetition is interesting to you. You wish you had thought about it when you wrote *Kinship and Performance in the Black and Green Atlantic* (Gough 2014). Yet, you don't know if you would know what to do with the material if you had thought about it. The book was written before your middle age and details a time long after the Middle Ages. And that book is about repetition. Whatever this is, it is about something else.

In *Kinship and Performance*, you begin with the story of Frederick Douglass, who, in 1845, escapes slavery on a ship called *The Cambria*. When those pro-slavery passengers discover he is a fugitive slave and threaten to throw him overboard, an Irish soldier, Capt. Thomas

Gough of the 33rd Foot, comes to his aid—threatening to toss overboard all those who are against Douglass. Thomas, it seems, is an early coconspirator.[2] In your book, you are thinking about how solidarity between the Irish and Black population on one side of the Atlantic (Ireland) turns into disavowal and active racism by the Irish on the other side (United States). But this Gough, this Capt. Thomas, unlike your Gough ancestors in Maryland who enslaved people in a state where Douglass escapes from bondage—this Gough is in the Atlantic gap, he is in the bardo, not in Ireland, not in America, he is white, but not quite.

You're thinking about how the very existence of your ancestors brings about the repeated patterns of trauma in your own family—patterns that are inextricably tied to America's traumatic underbelly; a repetition that is also an origin story. You're also thinking about how your very existence requires these ancestors to precede your own appearance on the world stage. You owe your life to them. "If only there were evil people somewhere insidiously committing evil deeds, and it were necessary only to separate them from the rest of us and destroy them," writes Aleksandr Solzhenitsyn, "but the line dividing good and evil cuts through the heart of every human being. And who is willing to destroy a piece of his own heart?" (1975: 168). What to do?

While you know you are not here to redeem your slaveholding ancestors, you also feel them with you, have felt them since you almost self-sabotaged and did not complete *Kinship and Performance in the Black and Green Atlantic*. You are sitting in your office on the other side of the Atlantic in Glasgow, Scotland (maybe the first Gough to reverse migrate since the 1650s), and you hear a voice that is very distinctly not your own voice say to you: *you must do this, you need this to heal.*

What does it mean to heal? How do we redeem our own lives? In your book, you don't feel the need to repeat (again) the story of the patriarchs. That is a history that gets you nowhere. Instead, your book is about women and children. If you are honest, there is one particular young woman who might be responsible for the whole project. She does not know this because you have not seen her since you were a pre-teen. You ride the school bus together. She lives two streets from you, and yet it is a different world. You share a last name. You attend the same church. You're not sure of your relationship. It puzzles you for at least a couple of years, and yet you also know that somehow you are not allowed to ask about it. Silence then, now, and in the future was always already an unnamed violence. Then one day in sixth or seventh grade—you can't remember—you are both sitting in a circle across from each other learning about the underground railroad and listening to a recording of someone singing the song that leads slaves to freedom: "Follow the Drinking Gourd."

What is it about song that unlocks memory? Without any discussion, just the sounds of the song, you understand something about whiteness that you will not be able to articulate until decades later. Whiteness is something that terrorizes, something that you try to escape even at the risk of your own life. You understand that what is being sung at that moment is not about you, and not *not* about you. Whose ancestral trauma are you hearing? Is it from the ancestors who look like you, or the ones who look like P, both who carry the same last name?

Recently you went searching for P online to see if she is still living in the same town where you knew her as a child. You type her name and the name of your small town into Google, but instead of a contemporary Black woman appearing on the screen, you see a black-and-white photograph of a white woman staring back at you. One of your dead relatives who is also the First Lady of Maryland from 1831 to 1833. A ghostly double of a woman you are not seeking, but who just might be seeking *you*.

***

By the end of the nineteenth century, one of theatre's "doubles" (that almost kills theatre) is made possible by the invention of daguerreotype and early photography: cinema. You tell me that at the fin de siècle everything theatrical is looking to photography and film for direction: actors on stage start pretending the audience is not there; audiences see actors play inside middle-class living rooms much like the ones they just left to go to the theatre; and the stage lighting that electricity makes possible also makes possible a certain kind of acting that—with the benefit of hindsight—seems less histrionic and grand, more of what is later referred to as "cinematic." In any case, the framing machinery that makes realism look like "reality" also depicts a particular kind of reality: it is white and middle class, and while realism is essentially a genre that co-arises with women's suffrage, it is really a genre best suited to represent the triumph of white men over pretty much everything. You genuinely wonder whether it is surprising that this genre has influenced our understanding of the theatrical and cinematic arts to such a degree that, to many people, it seems like it is not a genre at all, just a representation of "real life."

Early in the twentieth century, there are already many theatre artists and theorists who rail against realism in the theatre. Recently you re-read Antonin Artaud's *The Theatre and Its Double* (1958) for a class you are teaching. It is such an odd, brutal, compelling collection of essays on Artaud's thoughts and propositions for what theatre should be. At one point he suggests it should be more like the plague (in an essay aptly entitled "The Theatre and the Plague"). There is no middle way for Artaud. The middle way, or the middle class and their bourgeois theatre in any case, is the problem. You're certainly not in love with Artaud's theories and agree with him about little. However, given your own compulsion to think through doubles, and the double relations that appear to be a kind of cruel theatre in your own ancestry, his most important theory, "The Theatre of Cruelty," seems vital to consider.

First, you tell me that it might be important to understand that, for Artaud, the theatre's double is kind of like a Jungian shadow—the repressed, the unconscious, the abject. Also, Artaud thinks that theatre can and should work differently than other mediums that are obsessed with lifelikeness (like cinema, like photography, like sculpture). You agree with him on this point. You think that if every theatre in the entire world never produced another play in the genre of realism, the world and the theatre would be a better place. You take your lead from the poet and critic Nathaniel Mackey who has expressed it better than anyone you've heard: "the refusal to represent experience in an acceptably reductive, realist manner, proceeds from a gnostic estrangement from the world that realism wants to portray" (Mackey 1978: 635–6).

Gnostic estrangement becomes a kind of mantra for you. You wonder if this describes your own distrust when it comes to realism as a genre—its reductive nature, its focus on a kind of material reality that lacks substance, and which does not feel true for you. Your knowledge of the world and your embodied experience in the world suggests the crude limitations of realism to express reality. You want to return to this, but first you want to read aloud Artaud's words in his essay "No More Masterpieces":

> I am not one of those who believe that civilization has to change in order for the theater to change; but I do believe that the theater, utilized in the highest and most difficult sense possible, has the power to influence the aspect and formation of things… That is why I propose a theater of cruelty. With this mania we all have for depreciating everything, as soon as I have said "cruelty," everybody will at once take it to mean "blood." But "*theater of cruelty*" means a theater difficult and cruel for myself first of all. And, on the level of performance, it is not the cruelty we can exercise upon each other by hacking at each other's bodies, carving up personal anatomies, or, like Assyrian emperors, sending parcels of human ears, noses, or

neatly detached nostrils through the mail, but much more terrible and necessary cruelty which things can exercise against us. We are not free. And the sky can still fall on our heads. And the theater has been created to teach us that first of all. (1958: 79)

You like that Artaud turns theater inside-out, uses it as a way of thinking about life and what falls outside of the frame, what constitutes this double that he wants to present on stage (which, ultimately is unrepresentable). You reflect on doubles in your own family's history: the brave Capt. Thomas Gough who helps Frederick Douglass aboard *The Cambria* is some kind of "good" double to your ancestors in St. Mary's County, Maryland, who own a plantation where people are enslaved during the same era. In another theatre of cruelty, it is precisely how many records are archived regarding the "reality" of your ancestors that eclipses your childhood classmate's ancestors' history at the same time and in the same location, paradoxically making *her* the double, the repressed, or the unrelated relation. This is Mackay's gnostic estrangement writ large across something called "American History."

***

It is when you go searching for another Thomas, one more ancient than Capt. Thomas who comes to Douglass's aid, that you stumble upon a text that demonstrates the crude limitations of realism by sheer contrast: "I who write this am Thomas, the Double, the Twin. Yeshua [Jesus], the Living Master, spoke, and his secret sayings I have written down. I assure you, whoever grasps their meaning will not know the taste of death" (Bauman 2003: 5). These words begin the gnostic Gospel of Thomas discovered in Upper Egypt near the town of Nag Hammadi by Muhammad Ali al-Samman in December 1945. Found in a group of thirteen papyrus books bound in leather inside a red earthenware jar about three feet high, scholars now date these Coptic texts to AD 350–400, or roughly 300–400 years after Jesus's physical death.

You cannot quite remember how you found this text, but you remain interested because of this announcement of his doubleness. Like a Zen koan, Thomas wants his readers to find out for themselves what this twin-ship might mean to them. In the original Coptic text, the name Thomas is mentioned twice—once in Greek and once in Aramaic, emphasizing the meaning of his name as "the Double," and "the Twin" (Bauman 2003: 6). While there is something quite literal about this announcement, you wonder why the scribe of Jesus's secret teachings writes the meaning of his own name twice if this is not also a code for another way of knowing—a gnostic estrangement from a reductive depiction of reality that signals that all is not as it appears.

You listen into the gap and feel the astonishing alienation between this Thomas speaking to you from a text written over 1,500 years ago, and the Thomas you think you know, the biblical persona simply known as "Doubting Thomas." In one version of Thomas's story, he is the one who is incredulous and must rely entirely on physical proof as evidence of something that seems to defy all probability. In his "double" life, the one that remains hidden until it is found in the desert in North Africa in 1945, he is a writer and the keeper of a gnostic lineage that—far from not believing that Jesus can rise from the dead—tells the reader that if they come to understand these teachings, they will not know the taste of death. Does Thomas understand these teachings? You wonder if Thomas ever tastes death. You think back to the performance artist. She once performed a piece called *Lips of Thomas*.[3] Does she taste death, or do the lips reveal Thomas's secret?

You say that Thomas is the most theatrical of saints, one who announces his doubleness at the beginning of book about nonduality.[4] You get the impression that the dictates of realism have ensured that Thomas, the actor, *becomes* the "Doubting Thomas" character. You are uncertain what to think about doubt since you, yourself, are so prone to doubt. Is doubting your reality such a bad thing? Is it opposed to wisdom or is it a doorway? Thomas's double life gives you

Figure 6.1. Caravaggio, *The Incredulity of Saint Thomas*, Florence, Italy, 1601.

tools for getting at the depth of the surface story (Bal 1999: 27), for listening into the gap where you may feel your way into reality by another route.

You recall Caravaggio's *Incredulity of Thomas* (1601; see figure 6.1), the dramatic painting of his interpretation of the story of Thomas as recorded in the Gospel of John. In John's authorized version of the story, Thomas protests that "until I see in Jesus's hands the print of the nails and put my finger in the place of the nails, and put my hand into his side, I will not believe" (John 20:25). Then Jesus appears—to Thomas and two other disciples—and comes up with the goods. He directs Thomas to "put your finger here; see my hands. Reach out your hand and put it into my side. Stop doubting and believe" (John 20:27). You remember how Caravaggio depicts the play of hands between Thomas and Jesus. In this baroque, proto-cinematic painting, Caravaggio shows Thomas putting his finger directly into a wound in the side of Christ's body; indeed, you see Jesus *directing* his hand to touch the wound. What does this touch really verify? "To what extent can we put our faith in the certainty of the hand's touch? What can and cannot be known from touch, and what are its epistemological limitations?" (Levi 2021: 32).

Since your own series requires you to follow hands into another way of knowing, these questions feel urgent. Yet, you can't say that these hands have put your doubt to rest. While Caravaggio's painting allows you to think faith and doubt together, you wonder if he is also wrestling with what the hands, and touch, really mean without quite resolving the issue. The story of Caravaggio using his genius for physical naturalism as an argument of faith (Creighton 1995: 152) is the story of how seeing as a way of believing has been the privileged way of knowing since the Renaissance. And yet, when you scratch the surface, you find that things are not quite as they appear. His use of chiaroscuro, the play of shadow and light, reveals a kind of hyperrealism—it is a *theatrical* painting. Jesus directs Thomas's fingers into a bloodless wound as if he is being directed to touch a theatrical body. What kind of knowledge is gained by touching a body returned to life as theatre? In fact, this entire painting seems to be painted from the point of view of the bloodless wound that is held under a kind of spotlight where all eyes are directed. Caravaggio's painting begs you to ask if this is the knowledge you think it is or does it take you somewhere else.

Another clue that this baroque reality exceeds the genre of realism comes in the depiction of the disciples themselves: red noses, torn garments, dirty fingernails. Caravaggio does not depict some ancient reality; instead, these men are his contemporaries. He records people he sees in the streets and incorporates them into his work. While his contemporary critics found this lazy and artless, you wonder if these too-defensive critiques are pointing to the ways that Caravaggio *challenges* the realism of his era. Mieke Bal (1999), writing about

Caravaggio, tells you, "Illusionism is an excess of representation that undoes representation, and that might well, we can now wonder, undo reality as such" (1999: 42). The artist forces the viewer of the image to meditate on this scene, to see what can only be described as the gap— between past and present, classicism and the baroque, between reality and illusion, between seeing and touching, and between life and a dream. Not only that, if his contemporaries can be folded into the Thomas story through their hands (in all of their dirty, gritty detail), then how might your hands be reaching for these theatrical hands as a way of accessing a double mystery. In the "baroque point of view," writes Bal, "subjectivity and the object become co-dependent, folded into one another, and this puts the subject at risk" (1999: 28).

You feel the risk is that reality is now more porous, more relational, must include both the theatre and its double. Even a theatrical touch can radically upend what you know to be true. Caravaggio is often quoted as saying, "reality is my teacher," and there's no doubt in your mind that it teaches him many things. Reality, of course, is not the genre of realism. Reality is more real than the mere representation of lifelikeness, more prone to mystery, contingency, relationality, and less prone to hierarchy. You wonder if Caravaggio is painting hands onto this material surface to point to something that cannot, literally, be grasped. One of the secret teachings in Thomas's gnostic gospel seems to echo the theatrical reality Caravaggio renders on canvas: "Jesus said to them, 'When you make the two into one, and when you make the inner like the outer and the outer like the inner, and the upper like the lower, and when you make male and female into a single one, so that the male will not be male nor the female be female, when you make eyes in place of an eye, a hand in place of a hand, a foot in place of a foot, an image in place of an image, then you will enter [the (Father's) domain]'" (Bauman 2003: 51–2).

Reality makes room for alienation and estrangement, it makes room for the mystery that stands in between Thomas and his Double, the keeper of a secret wisdom tradition who is full of doubt. This gap makes space for the possibility that both can be real, or that both are one, or like Caravaggio's contemporary who stands in as Thomas in his painting, that you, too, are Thomas.

Notes

1 For a partial list of critical works that examine this history from different angles, see Allen (1994), Baucom (2005), Douglass (1950), Gilroy (1993), Hartman (1997), Ignatiev (1995), James (1938), Lott (1995), Patterson (1982), Spiller (1987), Wells-Barnett ([1892] 2002), Williams (1944), and Young (2010).
2 See "The Cambria Riot" in Douglass ([1845] 1979). For a digital copy, see <https://glc.yale.edu/cambria-riot-my-slave-experience-and-my-irish-mission> accessed June 19, 2023; see also Fenton (2014).
3 Abramović performed *Lips of Thomas* (1975) in Innsbruck, Austria, and again at the Guggenheim in New York as a part of *Seven Easy Pieces* (2005). For more details, see < https://www.li-ma.nl/lima/catalogue/art/marina-abramovic/lips-of-thomas-1975-2005/9370 > accessed February 3, 2023.
4 Curiously, this Thomas who is discovered in a desert in 1945, and who writes down the oral teachings of Jesus (i.e., he is Jesus's scribe), does so 1,000 years before the medieval Scrivener's guild (i.e., a guild of scribes) enact the *Incredulity of Thomas* during York's Corpus Christi cycle.

Lecture 7

Duende, or Play and Death

A couple years ago you dream that you are reentering a classroom you recently left. As you walk toward the doorway, you see the back of a woman who appears to be hanging in the doorframe. You know the woman in the door is dead. When you enter the classroom and turn around to look at her, however, you see she is not hanging but floating. Even still, she is most definitely dead. Her appearance in the doorway seems both generous and mysterious. She has light brown hair and her piercing blue eyes are wide open. She is wearing red. All red: dress, scarf, lipstick. She is dressed like a cross between a Flamenco dancer and the medieval art historic depictions of Mary Magdalene dressed in the red robes of love, of sacrifice, of charity. When you look in a dream-mirror, you, too, are dressed like a Flamenco dancer, but in a black dress with a red scarf.

"All that has black sounds has *duende*," writes Federico Garcia Lorca (2010: 57). Lorca gave a lecture in Havana in 1933 called "Theory and Play of the Duende." You think about this lecture often because *duende*—which defies translation—is located at that thin place between performance and death, between creativity and obliteration. Like the color red, with its associations of blood, of passion, of new life, and of death, *duende* indicates that medial place between the life force and the death drive. It also came to mind because in the lecture Lorca discusses Flamenco. This is what he writes: "Think of the case of Saint Teresa, that supremely 'flamenco' woman who was so filled with duende. 'Flamenco' not because she caught a bull and gave it three magnificent passes (which she did!) ... but because she was one of those few creatures whose duende—not angel, for the angel never attacks—transfixed her with a dart and wanted to kill her for having stolen his deepest secret, the subtle bridge that unites the five senses with the raw wound, that living cloud, the stormy ocean of timeless love" (2010: 68).

The "duende's arrival always means a radical change in forms," writes Lorca, and you wonder what the dream woman's arrival means for your own changed form. Duende is associated with a heightened, amplified quality of the life force: those who possess it, or are possessed by it, are acutely aware of how precarious that force really is because it also longs to reconnect, to return to everything that is outside of it. Somewhere in the middle of this essay, Lorca writes, "Angel and Muse escape with violin, meter, and compass; the duende wounds. In the healing of that wound, which never closes, lie the strange, invented qualities of a [wo]man's work" (2010: 67). You think again of Thomas and wonder if Caravaggio's wound resembles the one to which Lorca refers.

Inside your dream, you stare at the woman for a long time, and she stares back out of her piercing blue eyes. You then flip through a book that depicts unusual paintings of geometric shape and color. You ask the woman if she can explain her artwork to you. She just blinks. Then, you walk through a wall, put on a formal blue coat (like a coat worn by an eighteenth-century solider) and jump onto a white horse that is among many other white horses trotting down a wide boulevard in what seemed to be a royal ceremonial parade. You must go slow and be very quiet. Soon, you dismount your horse and return to the artist. She is still floating in the door staring at the parade outside. With an emotional intensity that surprises you, you tell her that you love her paintings. She seems pleased and asks you to describe the paintings to which you might be referring. You do not know; you have no intimate knowledge of her work. You just know that you love it. The dream ends before your conversation can continue.

When you wake up, you write down what you remember. Aside from what you are wearing and where she is located, your first recollection is flipping through the book of paintings. You search for images of the work, and you see an image of your dream lady staring back at you from your iPad: Hilma af Klint (1862–1944). She is having a retrospective at the Guggenheim Museum in New York City: *Hilma af Klint: Paintings for the Future* (2018–19). An article you later read confirms that her eyes are, in fact, a piercing blue. When you verify Hilma's identity, the blue coats, the white horses, and the wide boulevard seem obvious signs of a Swedish royal ceremonial parade. Is it significant that you later read that her studio at the Royal Academy of Art in Stockholm overlooks the King's Garden, or that you are part of the parade? You do not know. Perhaps it is just a dream-time clue that this time, the flamenco *duende*-filled mystic is from Stockholm. Like Teresa of Avila, Hilma af Klint knows the secret of the "subtle bridge that unites the five senses with the raw wound, that living cloud, the stormy ocean of timeless love" (2010: 68).

※※※

Hilma af Klint is born in Solna, Sweden, the fourth child to Captain Victor af Klint, a Swedish naval commander, and Mathilda af Klint (née Sonntag). The family history, recorded in *The Af Klint Family* (1905), includes a title page designed by Hilma. The page depicts the family coat of arms surrounded by objects symbolizing the careers of most men in her family: a compass, a canon, a marine chart, an anchor, and a sailing vessel (Voss 2018: 49–63). Like her father, Hilma's grandfather and great grandfather are both officers in the Swedish navy. She is forty-three years old when the book is published and on the verge of entering the most prolific artistic period of her life. Unlike her celebrated patriarchal lineage, however, it is in 2013, almost one hundred years after Hilma begins her *Paintings for the Temple*—193 astonishing paintings that she makes between the years 1906 and 1915—that she is celebrated in a retrospective at the Moderna Museet in Stockholm. This modern art museum is a mile from the Royal Academy of Fine Art where she is one of the first women to gain entrance in 1882, at the age of twenty.

From the very beginning of her artistic career, Hilma has a dual interest in science and spirituality. While the trajectory from her early work through to the beautiful and radical abstractions for which she is known to you in the twenty-first century is well documented, there is little about the paintings that she begins in her 40s that can be predicted by exploring her early work. Trained in traditional drawing and painting, she is an accomplished illustrator and exacting painter. She makes botanical drawings, paints landscapes, contributes illustrations to scientific journals, and paints portraits on commission. Her work is so highly regarded that she is given a free studio in which to work at the Royal Academy of Fine Art.

In 1879, caught up in the current of her time, Hilma becomes fascinated in spiritualism and mediumship. When her much loved sixteen-year-old sister dies the following year, her dedication to conversing with the spirit world intensifies. Unlike the fin de siècle faddishness of spiritualism in general, Hilma's interest is lifelong. In 1896, she starts holding regular meetings with four other women who called themselves The Five (De Fem). While this, too, may be incidental, you are struck by a certain mathematical symmetry—Hilma af Klint is the last of the five artist-mystics—following Hildegard of Bingen, Eleonora Duse, Simone Weil, and Marina Abramović—who calls out to you in some mysterious way, persuading you to think with her for a while. Of course, there is also the strange resonance with your playlet with Pythagoras where you discuss five as a number associated with regeneration: five never begins or ends but keeps coming back to where it starts.

From 1896 to 1907, The Five keep five notebooks to describe their meetings with detailed descriptions. The women take the practice of contacting the spirit world very seriously. They record their experiences, describe their encounters, carry out automatic writing and drawing, and note their meetings with the "High Masters," the name they give to the spirits with whom they converse (Muller-Westermann 2018: 14).

During the decade that Hilma meets and conducts séances with her Spiritualist companions, her reputation as a well-respected figurative painter continues to rise. In 1906, after a decade of meeting with The Five, her interest in science, evident in her botanical and veterinary paintings, as well as in her illustrations for scientific journals, braids itself with her spiritual calling. While sitting with The Five during a séance on January 1, 1906, Amaliel, the name of one of the "High Masters" with whom they conversed, asks the women to extend their work undertaken in the circle to a series of full-fledged paintings. Fearing that so much direct contact with the spirit world would cause madness, all the women decline, except Hilma af Klint. She records in one of her notebooks that "Amaliel offered me a commission and I immediately replied: yes. This became the great commission, which I carried out in my life" (qtd in Bashkoff 2018: 20).

***

You arrive at the Guggenheim Museum for Af Klint's retrospective and immediately encounter the work that you remember asking her to explain to you in your dream without knowing what it is: *The Ten Largest* (1907; see Figure 7.1), a series of paintings that stand at a height of more than three meters.[1] The series can only be described as mind stopping. Af Klint creates each painting over four days with no models, diagrams, or notes. In one of the many notebooks Hilma af Klint kept over the course of her life, she writes that the *Paintings for the Temple* "were painted directly through me, without any preliminary drawings, and with great force. I had no idea what the paintings were supposed to depict; nevertheless, I worked swiftly

Figure 7.1. An employee poses with a series entitled *The Ten Largest* (1907). L–R: No. 6, Adulthood; No. 7, Adulthood; No. 8, Adulthood; and No. 10, Old Age by Hilma af Klint as part of the Serpentine Galleries' Spring Exhibition in central London on March 2, 2016. Photo credit Ben Stansall/AFP via Getty Images.

and surely, without changing a single brush stroke" (qtd in Horowitz 2018: 128).

Using tempera paint, the creamy consistency flowing smoothly onto the large areas of paper that she glued together and affixed to canvas, it is clear from footprints found in the paint, that at least some (if not all) of the paintings were completed on the ground—an unprecedented way of making art at the time. What she creates is so astonishing that there is hardly any noise from the gallery visitors the day you are there. When you show the images of the paintings to your friends afterward, they remark on how they feel as if the paintings are trying to communicate, how the paintings might actually be speaking. This is certainly the feeling you have when you go to view them a second time during your seven-hour gallery visit. You simply sit with the paintings and listen.

In the later years of her life, Hilma af Klint studies her paintings and takes copious notes on the possible meanings. She also keeps glossaries helping to decipher the symbology of her work as a whole. In one of these entries, she gives the "backstory" of Amaliel, the High Master who gives her this commission. She notes that he "[f]ormerly lived in Tibet but now serves on the spiritual plane and has reached a point in his evolution where he now understands the secrets of the astral world. Is faithful, humble, wise" (Af Klint 2018: 255).

After reading that Amaliel, the "High Master" who gave Hilma af Klint her commission, is from Tibet, you instinctively grab a copy of Chogyam Trungpa's *True Perception: The Path of Dharma Art* (2008) from your bookshelf. A former Tibetan monk and founder of the Shambhala lineage in the United States (the first manifestation that is located in Vermont, not far from where you now live), Chogyam Trungpa's book is a compilation of a series of Dharma Art lectures he gave in the 1970s. Beginning with the first sentence of the first lecture included in the collection, he tells you that the "term *dharma art* does not mean art depicting Buddhist symbols or ideas ... Rather, dharma art refers to art that springs from a certain state of mind on the part of the artist that could be called the meditative state. It is an attitude of directness and unself-consciousness in one's creative work" (emphasis in the original; 2008: 1). You think that this perfectly encapsulates how Hilma af Klint describes her own creative process while working on *Paintings for the Temple*. After reading this sentence, you flip through his book and quickly stop on a lecture devoted to the subject of individuality entitled, "Choiceless Magic."

Chogyam Trungpa begins by explaining how "it is very difficult to get hold of one's individuality." He says that "spiritually or otherwise, we do not trust our individuality, and that is one of our biggest problems" (2008: 109). In the West, and particularly in the United States, which is founded on the myth of rugged individualism, this statement may seem confusing. When it comes right down to it, however, it is very difficult for human beings to operate outside of tribal consciousness (whether you call this tribe family influence, religious influence, peer pressure, career pressure, cultural, societal, and political norms). "Whenever there is a break from conventionally accepted channels of thought, we get frightened," writes Chogyam Trungpa, "we try to avoid our individuality and instead emulate something else" (2008: 110–11).

You tell me that you will only speak for yourself when you say that despite what it might look like at this point in the lecture series, you very much try to avoid your own individuality for almost four decades. Individuality is there regardless, but when you look around, it might be possible to notice when people are living inside a story that is not completely of their making (maybe this even describes you). Having grown up in a very traditional household, you unconsciously hold onto patterns of the way you *think* you should be living your life, even when these patterns do not seem to make those to whom you model your life very happy. What you know is that you long to be "normal" (whatever that means), and you are hell bent on your life looking "normal" whatever the cost to your physical, psychological, and spiritual health. Why this is the case for so many years is a bit of a mystery. You have theories about addiction and about childhood trauma—all your transgenerational inheritances—but somehow just before middle age, you admit defeat. You simply cannot play by the rules anymore. So, you surrender to your life, and the rules of the game begin to change.

Ultimately, you do not think it is all that relevant how you get to a place of surrender—whether your story begins in a difficult childhood, addiction, accident, trauma, spiritual experience, or any of the ten thousand joys or ten thousand sorrows. It only matters that at some point in your life that you get there. If you are still paying attention to this lecture series, chances are you already know this. Have you already said "yes, I surrender," or are you doing so in serial installments? It makes no difference. At some point there's only "yes." That is the "choiceless magic" Chogyam Trungpa is discussing.

"We all have our own style and our own particular nature," writes Chogyam Trungpa. "We can't avoid it." As if speaking directly to the paintings of Hilma af Klint, he says, "the enlightened expression of yourself is in accord with your inherent nature. ... There is a basic iconographic pattern in the universe, like the existence of the seasons and the elements, but how we react to that is individual" (2008: 111). Outwardly, and for a very long time, Hilma af Klint lives her life as a traditional painter. In this version of herself, her role as artist is to use the paintbrush in her hand to depict the life she finds in nature (of plants, trees, flowers, landscapes, animals, portraiture). She does so with incredible accuracy so that the paintings are held up as models of painterly technique or illustrate scientific studies. Painting is a means to an end.

This phase of her artistic vocation preoccupies her life from her entrance to the Royal Academy of Fine Art at twenty years old and persists into her early forties. Then, there is a profound shift: she completes her *Paintings for the Temple* in 1915, and never returns to figurative painting. From her middle age, her paintings are completed using a different consciousness; she operates from a different understanding of reality. In the first reality, her method of working is via direct observation of the physical world. In the second reality, her method is to make the invisible world behind her eyes visible via paint, paper, and canvas.

If one thinks only of what is depicted in her early "nature" paintings versus her later abstract paintings, then the dual aspects of visible and invisible, material and nonmaterial realities may seem like two sides of the same coin. But the shift is more profound than that. The medium of painting, itself, is employed for two radically different purposes. In the traditional paradigm, the painting method comes with a series of formal, disciplinary conditions: it is used to replicate reality that you see with your eyes, and to demonstrate technique. The study of painting is understood as contributing to the growth of the artistic medium, and to the history of art. In this paradigm, painting is employed with a particular end goal in mind, and those goals are codified by the tribe of experts. In other words, they are socially conditioned.

Like af Klint, you also receive traditional training. In your case, in the academic and creative fields of English, theatre, and performance studies. You devote most of your adult life to training students in particular techniques of research and practice. In some major respects, these are techniques that you are paid to teach to students. To enter the professional field at any level, there are methods, content, styles, techniques, and ways of thinking that must be carefully crafted and honed. During the first two decades of your academic life, until your early forties, you think your job is to illuminate how plays represent social reality, and how to best use the techniques of theatre to manifest that reality on the stage. You are convinced that the study and research of theatre and performance contribute to a greater understanding of the cultural and social world—past and present—in front of your eyes. In this paradigm, theatre is employed with a particular end goal in mind. Those goals are also codified by a tribe of experts who subscribe to socially conditioned rules about the art and craft of performance and theatre research.

Unlike the work Hilma af Klint produced in the first half of her life, in the second half of her life, the method she uses to create her radical abstract paintings illuminates a *process*. In part, this is clear in the way she paints in series, and *only* in series. Hilma af Klint's serial ordering is her way of manifesting the spiritual world, or her relationship with her higher self, or God, or the universe (which, in essence, are all One for Hilma). Paradoxically, it is through serial ordering based around thematical paintings where she seeks to demonstrate the nature of nonduality: the theory of Oneness that she believes is the True reality behind what is seen in our dualistic universe. The point is not to make "good art." It is also not to make "bad art." The abstract paintings that are her most unique contributions to art are, paradoxically, a vehicle and not the destination. In Simone Weil's language, painting is her *métaux*, the bridge she crosses to connect the material world in front of her eyes to the vast invisible world behind her eyes. The purpose is not to demonstrate technique or contribute to art history, but to give you knowledge about the reality that you cannot see, a knowledge that comes from the very edge of the known world. What she reveals is unique, but it is not *particular*. What is strikingly paradoxical about individuality is that the more you are yourself, the more you come into connection with the patterns of other human beings.

Resonant with Hilma af Klint, in your early forties you also become interested in using the techniques of your own training to illuminate a process. In this process, the tools of theatre and performance studies are not directed at honing the techniques for better stage practice but are the tools toward which you can build a transformative life practice. You think of these lectures as a culmination of your own serial thinking, a way of understanding how you can manifest your potential Self, the one who might be waiting in the wings for you to arrive to the story of your life.

This change in direction and intention, a change in where artistic work is leading and how you might get there, effectively made Hilma af Klint (and not painting) into the medium. It is no longer about the medium of painting per se, yet she cannot reach her higher self without it. Painting is Hilma's way into the mystery, just as performance is yours. Once she steps out of the world of her artistic tribe, and steps away from the methods, goals, and intentions assigned to artists, she is not recognized. She always knows this will be the case.

For a long time, you pay careful attention to Hilma af Klint's courageous and liberating decision to dismantle her own academic training. This is by no means to suggest that there is some binary divide between creative life and intellectual curiosity. Far from it. You are sure Af Klint would agree that anti-intellectual prejudice is the end of creative life. Her dismantling returns you to a question that you first ask when you go searching for Hildegard of Bingen: What does it mean to undo your training? For you, and for Hilma af Klint, undoing a lifetime of disciplinary training is not about throwing everything out the window. It is about what it might be to imagine asking your life—the one that wants to live through you—what you're here to learn at this moment. You think that this might mean taking professional ambition off the table—not because it is no longer possible, and not because you heroically must give up your desire to have your work make a splash in the world. It is off the table because it is the least important aspect of what you're here to do, which is, namely, to open yourself up to your own individuality. You are here to get out of your own way.

There is a built-in paradox to being a member of a community regardless of whether that community is some family configuration (biological or otherwise), a professional body, or a spiritual or religious faith. As a human being, you crave community, and often thrive in communities where you feel supported. At the same time, you cannot be a member of community without surrendering a good deal of your energy toward the group. Sometimes this is fantastic, but it can also lead to feeling confined, especially when your direct experience of what you know to be true for yourself contrasts with what the community wants you to be for their purposes.

Hilma af Klint's relationship to The Five ensures her a community where she can practice her intuitive and creative gifts among like-minded women. It is through the support of a strong spiritual community that she is then able to say yes to the "spiritual commission," and trust the messages that she receives from the "High Masters." Yet, her desire to head into the wilderness on her own despite the other women warning her against it illuminates the push and pull of community. You need to keep a balance between when you need community and when you need to forgo it to search inside for what you know is true. Like the story of Jesus appearing to Mary Magdalene alone in the garden, the challenge is that no one will be able to verify your truth for you. There will always be that aspect of you that, like Thomas, wants the certainty of your faith tested in the company of others who can confirm it for you. Accepting your own individuality means, ultimately, trusting yourself even when you will certainly fail, or make the wrong decision, or be told that your truth is unacceptable in some way. That's also part of the contract.

In one of af Klint's last notebooks, she requests that her artwork not be displayed in public until twenty years after her death. While this is a surprising request, it took far longer for her abstract paintings to appear in the public realm. While a handful of her paintings are exhibited at the Los Angeles County Museum of Art in 1986,[2] her first retrospective takes place at the Moderna Museet in Stockholm, *Hilma af Klint: A Pioneer of Abstraction* (2013). This is followed by the retrospective curated at the Serpentine Gallery in London, *Hilma af Klint: Painting the Unseen* (2016); then the curated exhibition at the Guggenheim in New York: *Hilma af Klint: Paintings for the Future* (2018–19). With six hundred thousand visitors, her Guggenheim exhibition is the most highly attended in the gallery's history. Hilma af Klint finally finds the future audience she seeks. It is while ascending the spiral path of the Guggenheim Museum, a path hundreds of thousands of others also travel to see her, that you first find yourself in her story, and then find yourself in your own.

***

Hilma af Klint's Vision of the World: Notes for a Performative Lecture

You can't put a frame around a ghost. It's a funny thought because the dream lady wearing a flamenco red dress, who is most definitely dead, is floating in a door frame that's leading into an art studio. So, I guess you can put a frame around it.

This reminds me of a terrible academic interview I had in London back in 2009. One professor, speaking of something I recently published, is visibly angry. She says, "It's just *so, so, so uncontainable.*" I want to say, "It's an essay on historical haunting, it's not a policy document. Of course it's uncontainable. You can't contain a goddamn ghost!" But this has always been my deal with academia. It's always wanting to contain the thing I want to set free.

I beg the dead dream lady to teach me about her art. She only blinks and smiles because she knows well before I do that her art cannot be taught. Her flamenco red dress reminds me of Federico Garcia Lorca's "Theory and Play of the Duende," of that fantastically untranslatable Spanish word. A mysterious force that everyone feels but no philosopher has explained. Lorca's essay suggests that the best of artists banish skill and safety so that they can play in that thin space, that lacuna, between the visible and invisible worlds. "The duende does not come at all unless he sees that death is possible," writes Lorca (2010: 67).

Three months after this dream, I'm at the Arthur Findlay College of Psychic and Mediumship Studies on the outskirts of London. I take an intensive week-long course on the foundations of mediumship. I'm not sure Hilma sent me, exactly, but I know more about what it means to play with death, or play in that thin space, that lacuna, which is, I think she would agree, creativity's birthplace. What I learn from the activities in which I participate is that we are all interconnected to an alarming degree. We pick up on stories, moods, thoughts, feelings, and memories of others whether we know it or not. Our unconscious is processing a hell of a lot of material that our egoic rational mind either misses or is not interested in decoding because it has little to do with who we think we are. You don't have to attend a course on mediumship to love Hilma af Klint's work. No self-respecting academic would suggest such a thing. But I am not interested in what is contained in her art; I want to know what she's setting free.

At the Guggenheim, I'm transfixed by *The Ten Largest* (1907)—a project that simultaneously undoes her training and unmakes art history in the process. Creating each painting of more than three meters over four days between October and December 1907, the series depicts the four stages of a human life (childhood, youth, adulthood, and old age). It is mind-stoppingly beautiful.

In the Guggenheim, the paintings surround the viewer from three sides and suggest a kind of immersion between the viewer and the world of the paintings. If we think of them as music, we can play the patterns in the paintings in real time. When we walk into this first gallery and encounter *The Ten Largest*, we walk into the Story of our Lives. This is not to be confused with small "s" story. The Story of our Lives that af Klint paints is the only one we share as a species. And the only thing we know about it is that it is a mysterious ride for all of us. The content, the form, and the spatial arrangement of the paintings all indicate that, despite the titles, there is not a past you and a future you. They are all you, all at once. They are life understood as surround-sound. Standing or sitting in front of *The Ten Largest*, the presence of nonmaterial reality is palpable. As a visitor viewing the paintings, you quickly realize they are pointing to something both profound and unsettling: we are confronted with the unknown in us, our unconditioned selves, all our light that we cannot see.

Imagine being Hilma af Klint in 1906 and saying "yes" to a spiritual commission from a "High Master" who "understands the secrets of the astral world" when you know that others will most likely think that you are batshit crazy (in fact, even the four women she works with in a mediumistic way think saying "yes" will bring about madness). Imagine what it might be to paint using techniques that are not known or discussed in artistic circles, even though you are one of only a few women trained in the most respected of these circles and receive accolades for demonstrating the techniques you honed so well. Imagine doing all this work knowing that it will not be accepted, and *still* absolutely knowing it is the most important work of your life, perhaps even the reason you incarnated as a human being at all. Now imagine doing this work without ever knowing that one hundred years later—well after you are gone—your work would be so influential that others would make a pilgrimage to see it, feeling the possibility of their own liberation because you had the courage to liberate yourself with such quirky, odd, awe-inspiring beauty. Would you say "yes"?

Once she steps out of the world of her artistic tribe, and steps away from the methods, goals, and intentions assigned to artists, she is not recognized by the academic community. She always knows this will be the case. She says "yes" because, unlike the other women who comprise The Five, she is more curious than afraid. With paintbrush in hand, she wants to know what potential unseen life she might be painting into existence.

For many months I wonder if she is teaching me a similar trick. Floating in the doorway in my dream, ready to watch me unmake my discipline and have the unmaking unmake me. I suspect that Hilma won't return to my dreamworld to answer this question for me. She knows, before I do, that I already understand what she is setting free, and knows, before I do, that I am already unmade and undone.

Notes

1 When af Klint began her *Paintings for the Temple* in 1906, the temple to which she refers did not exist, nor did one like it exist anywhere in the world. As Tracey Bashkoff (2018), the curator of af Klint's Guggenheim retrospective tells us, af Klint "envisioned her *Paintings for the Temple* filling a round building, where visitors would progress upward along a spiral path, on a spiritual journey defined by her paintings," which she

described in a 1931 notebook (2018: 17). The real synchronistic surprise of her temple as a spiral ascending upward, however, is that only a year earlier, in New York City, Hilla Rebay, who was also very interested in Spiritualism, began to conceptualize a building to house the abstract paintings that Solomon R. Guggenheim had been collecting under her advisement. Rebay imagined a museum built in "a fabulous style," one where there was a "room to rest in, a large space where the pictures are properly stored so that only a few are hung in sequence and only a few great artists are shown." She referred to this museum as the "temple of non-objectivity and devotion." "Temple," she remarked, "is nicer than church'" (qtd in Bashkoff 2018: 26). It took several decades for Rebay's vision of this artistic temple to take shape under the direction of Frank Lloyd Wright, America's foremost architect at the time. Charged by Rebay to create "a temple of spirit—a monument," Wright generated "a series of six design phases over sixteen years" (2018: 29). Wright's vision—which is the form the Guggenheim Museum takes today—is "a structure oriented around an unbroken spiral that rises more than six stories" (2018: 29).

2 About a dozen of af Klint's works were included in the Los Angeles County Museum of Art's *The Spiritual in Art: Abstract Painting 1890–1985* (1986), curated by Maurice Tuchman and Judi Freeman.

Lecture 8

Theatron, the Seeing Place

What does it mean to be unmade and undone, you wonder? It is the last lecture in the series, the last mystery play, so to speak, so you know you are at The Last Judgment. That is typically the theme of the play that concludes a medieval mystery cycle. You sense that this Last Judgment is less biblical fire and brimstone, and more personal reckoning. What you know at this point in the series is that mystery plays always speak in multiple languages, so it is impossible to say for sure.

A dream you have about three years ago really gets at this theme of being unmade. In it, you are in Glasgow climbing a timber staircase that appears newly built. At the top of the stairs is the apartment of a beloved friend. The confounding issue is that there is a large gap—a chasm, really—between the top stair and the apartment door. As you speak to your friend across this gap, you narrate to her that everything in the street below—convenience store, lottery ticket stand, deli, dry cleaner, all of it—is gone and someone is mopping the floor where all these things had been. The whole world outside, mopped away.

Sometime in the week following this dream, your friend calls you from across the pond while you are sitting in your office preparing a lecture. Stage four, she says. Not much time, she continues. In two months, your friend is dead. So much for bridging the gap. There exists a great chasm where once lived a quality of love you will likely never know in that way again.

Now you are re-reading *The End of Your World* (2008) by Adyashanti, a spiritual teacher. You come across a statement that has jarring resonance. He tells the reader that when you come to the end of your world (not corporeal death, but something like nonidentification with your ego), there is no new version of you, instead, he says, there is *no you*. Is this what it means to be unmade and undone? The whole world inside, mopped away?

You can't help but notice that the dreamworld visit to your friend's apartment appears to take place on a stage. It is as if a giant set is being dismantled by stagehands at the close of a production. In fact, the performance has had such a long run that it lulls you into believing in its permanence. This is what the stagehands remind you: that there is a reality always waiting in the wings when the lights go down for the last time. If you are the actor still left on stage, you are forced to relinquish your role. The deconstruction of your world by the stagehands leaves you no choice. All those hands that made up your world have a large role in unmaking it, too.

Now what?

The only thing you know for sure is that there is so much you do not know. As you stand in the middle of the empty stage after your world gets taken apart you have no idea where you are. No play-text, no theory book, no google directions, no compass, no map. You have no choice but to begin again right where you are.

You pay attention.

What do you notice? What is supporting you? The ground. The ground is supporting you. Good news. This means you are still in a body. There are so many bodies that you miss, but your body is not missing. It is right here.

Then what happens?

You go back to noticing how absence feels in your body. You notice, too, what it feels like to be in this expansive space all by yourself. When you notice, remember the ground. It will remind you that you have a body.

What do you hear in this space? Anything?

As you stand there feeling the ground beneath your feet, the breath coming in and out of your nostrils, the damp cool air on your skin, you also start to hear your own training waving at you like a ghost: "Adieu, adieu! Remember me!"

It appears, then it disappears, other times it remains, or is restored, or repeats itself, or is beyond repetition, or is mediated through other mediums. Whatever it is in theory, all you know is that you haven't been here before and that is both alarming and interesting.[1]

Is that it?

You begin again with your feet on the ground, and the breathing, and the paying attention, and then you wonder if you really *are* at the beginning? As you listen, you become aware that no performance theory can save you from the performance you are experiencing right now. The theories you are holding slip through your hands and dissolve.

So now you notice your hands. Like *really* notice. What do you see? Are they yours? Are you sure? It is here that you remember that it is time to play your final hand.

***

Close your eyes, or soften your gaze, and open yourself to the sounds around you. Hold up your left hand. Don't look at it yet. Just feel your left hand in the air. What do you know about your left hand? Maybe you never think about it, or maybe you are a lefty, so this hand is important to you. Think about what this hand allows you to do in your life each day, each moment, really. You, yourself, may have forgotten all about it if the ghost hand didn't wave at you, imploring you to remember.

Then you see it, the Guidonian Hand, dubiously named after the eleventh-century Benedictine monk, Guido of Arezzo (991/992— after 1033). You are introduced to this hand about a decade ago while reading *The Medieval Craft of Memory* (Carruthers and Ziolkowski

2002; see Figure I.1). This hand-y aide-memoire not only helps students to remember the order of notes in a given song, but it also helps you to remember overlapping relationships. It does so by turning something you hear into something you see. It makes the invisible world visible—a visual map of auditory space. What is remarkable is that you have this technology in your own hands. Having a hand gives everyone the capacity to make the invisible world visible. The hand makes your world shareable.

Return to your left hand and hold it up. Open and close your hand, notice the tips and joints of your fingers. Can you feel your thumb? How about your knuckles? On the Guidonian Hand, the musical notes are placed on the joints and tips of the fingers. Starting with the tip of your thumb, you read the musical notes in a spiral around the hand. Unlike in modern music where notes are simply understood as A, B, C, D, E, F, G and placed on a staff, like rungs on a ladder, on the Guidonian Hand, each tip and joint of your fingers carries not only a note name, but also its position in the hexachord system. This is how the hand helps you to remember both the order of notes and overlapping relationships.

You are thinking to yourself that this all seems very technical. You're not a musician. Why do you care about the notes? You're not sure. But you are interested in relationship, and this keeps you interested in the hand. The hand now feels like a cypher that you need to decode, but before you do, you want to understand its function in the Middle Ages. It just might be the kind of thing you need to remember in middle age. You wonder if this hand-y aide-memoire is helping you to remember time differently, gently taking *you* by the hand to guide you toward a way of entering times that are not seen but heard and felt.

Begin again at the tip of the thumb. This is the lowest note (think of it as the lowest C you can sing). Then go down to the base of the thumb and follow a spiral pattern around the hand. First across the base of the fingers, then up the pinky finger, across the tips of the fingers, down the pointer finger, across again at the lowest joint to the pinky, and then back across so the journey ends in the middle joint of the middle finger.

The image that is now in your hand is that of a spiral. Phi is in your hand, and in music, and in shell spirals, and pinecones, and flower petals, and the pyramids at Giza, and the Milky Way galaxy, and the shape of hurricanes, and the diameter of Saturn to its rings. Whatever is in the hand is in the world and whatever is in the world is in the hand. This is remarkable because if the hand is in the world and the world is in the hand, then your world has not been mopped away inside or outside. There is a reality you cannot see from your position on that stage, but you feel it through your hands. It is as real as music. This hand is how you access this world, how you bring it into reality. The hand teaches you to remember the world you cannot see because without it nothing can be made. The whole world can be played on your hand. The hand is always remembering relationships, is always shareable, that is its *modus operandi*.

This reminds you of the hexachord: a series of six notes that the hand teaches you to play in its three varieties (a natural hexachord begins with C, a hard hexachord begins with G, and a soft hexachord begins with F). Why is this important to your story? It may not be, but you like to include the details. The details tell you something, perhaps because of their relationship to your hands.

For instance, in the Middle Ages, to complete the whole gamut of formally recognized musical tones, you must learn a series of seven overlapping hexachords. You're amused by this fact because to complete your lecture series, your gamut, you also chart the movement of seven overlapping hands over the course of a series of seven lectures. This is how you know that while you only remember the Guidonian Hand here, in this last lecture, and only when you think everything is lost, it is with you from the beginning, always asking you to remember, to play it again until you learn about relatedness, relationships, and how you bring things into relation.

***

You are struck by the way Johannes Tinctoris, in his *Expositio manus*, or "Treatise on the Hand" (1477), describes the Guidonian Hand as a medium, as a "container for the contained." According to Tinctoris, "*any hand*, that extreme member placed at the end of the arm on the human body according to physiologists, contains that lesson in the tips and joints of its fingers" (my emphasis; Seay & Tinctoris 1965: 200). While he describes the hand as a medium, it is never stable as such. It is neither inside nor outside, form nor content, thought nor techne, but always working at the intersection of both. For Tinctoris, the hand is a representation of an outer teacher and simultaneously points you to your inner teacher. In essence, Tinctoris is telling you that everything you need is in your hands. The hand is the connecting point between two worlds. It is the archetype of transition *par excellence.*

As you reflect on the hands that you follow—from Hildegard of Bingen to Mary Magdalene, to Eleonora Duse, to Simone Weil, to Marina Abramović, to your ancestors' hands, to Hilma af Klint—all the way to your own hands, you are struck by another property of the Guidonian Hand: a property made visible by its absence. The Guidonian Hand has no time signature. It doesn't tell you about tempo, or rhythm, or whole and half notes; it doesn't teach you about 4/4 time, or 3/4 time, or any other time. It records nothing of time. The only time on the hand is the present. The hands of time? A misnomer.

You must admit, when you find these artists, or they come looking for you, you initially have no real interest. What you mean is that you do not much care about their biographical lives. Of course, you care a little, you care that they are *sui generis*, the first of their kind. But their lives do not resonate with you. What you mean is that you are not *personally* interested. Yet, you are compelled to pay close attention.

Later you see that you are compelled by their creative process. Why, you wonder? What is it teaching you? Even later you see that their creative process unmakes them. What you mean is that as they follow their discipline, surrender themselves entirely to their discipline, it takes them somewhere else, somewhere that they, *personally*, cannot predict or manufacture.

They are each a protagonist in their own mystery play. As they follow their discipline into the invisible world and carry what they discover back into the visible world and make it shareable, they begin to remake the world around them by introducing other possibilities. These possibilities are only partially visible through the products of their practice; what makes these products interesting is their relationship to the process of discovery.

Sharon Salzberg (2015), a meditation teacher and contributor to the "On Being" blog, writes about attending a discussion at Emory University entitled, "The Creative Journey: Artists in Conversation with the Dalai Lama on Spirituality and Creativity." In the discussion, the Dalai Lama is joined by Alice Walker and Richard Gere. Salzberg tells us that in the planning phase the panel members discussed the differences between Western and Eastern conceptions of artmaking, noting that "in the West many people believe that creativity comes from torment, whereas in the East there is a tradition of great art coming from balance and realization."

Salzberg writes that the Dalai Lama didn't understand the comparison, it made no sense to him. "In his view," she writes, "beautiful art was beautiful because of the inner transformation the artist went through during the act of creation. Did they become more enlightened, kinder, more deeply aware?" What makes art beautiful is the relationship between inside and outside. For the Dalai Lama you cannot know the beauty of a work of art until you understand how the consciousness of the creator is transformed in the process of making: they are always in relation.

You see in the Dalai Lama's reflection the source of your own torment: the thing that you are doing in and with theatre is not leading you to *that*. So, you start again with the hand, and it leads you to a place you cannot predict or manufacture. It takes you to a place that you do not know. You use the tools of your discipline hoping that if you can find a way to make the invisible, visible, that you can start to investigate the place where you are now. You write a series of lectures for a course that is never taught because the discipline in which they might be delivered does not exist. Will it ever exist? Is it even a discipline you're imagining here?

You don't know.

As an academic this is a very tricky place to be. As a human being, it is essential. There is a story—perhaps a Buddhist story, or an anticolonial story, or both, you can't remember—of the violence that comes from labeling and classifying. What happens when you look into the sky and see a thing with feathers that is flying, and instead of paying attention for yourself, you ask, "what is *that*?" You are quickly told it is a bird, so you stop looking at it because you know what it is now, so you think. Because you think you already know what it is you stop thinking with it, stop imagining its world, you stop paying attention.

What if instead you simply admit that you do not know what you are seeing? What if you think to yourself, what is it *really*—not as a word but as a life? What if you take your beginner's mind to your discipline and your Discipline? What if you take it to death and dying? What if you take it to your idea of who you are? What if you continue to live the questions in such a way that the questions think other questions, and these questions lead to stories, and these stories begin to tell other stories, and the stories start to build worlds inside the world you think you know until the world you think you know begins to pass away.

One of your teachers who helps you and your students to build worlds and understand them is Elinor Fuchs. Her essay "Visit to a

Small Planet: Questions to Ask a Play" (2004) helps students to imagine the world of the play as a small planet. Recently, you came across what you imagine is the invisible strata that runs through her world-building techniques. "My interest in eastern religion gives color to much of my work in theatre (and in life)," says Fuchs. "The essential task of life is the interweaving of two perceptions: one, the fundamental energy of existence is love; two, the fundamental nature of physical existence is impermanence. Developing the courage or wisdom to keep both alive, without extinguishing one for the other, is a life's work" ("Fuchs, Elinor [1933–]"). You are captivated by the way she imagines theatre as a loved one: making explicit how your job is to focus extreme attention on something that will be in front of you for a short period of time, and then disappear not to be repeated in the same way again. Not only that, but it is this tension between love and impermanence, play and death, *which keeps both alive.*

What if you start with love and impermanence? That is, you think, what Donna Haraway (2016) is asking you do it when she writes about "staying with the trouble" in her book by the same name. Haraway writes that she is inspired by the thinking of Marilyn Strathern, a British anthropologist and ethnographer of thinking practices, who teaches her that "it matters what stories we tell to tell other stories with; it matters what knots knot knots, what thoughts think thoughts, what descriptions describe descriptions, what ties tie ties. It matters what stories make worlds; what worlds make stories" (2016: 12). She also learns from Strathern (and you learn from Haraway) that you must accept the "risk of relentless contingency," of putting "relations at risk with other relations, from unexpected other worlds" (2016: 12). In a lecture given before the publication of *Staying with the Trouble* she issues a kind of rallying crying that, in part, you are attempting to imagine here: "it matters to destabilize worlds of thinking with other worlds of thinking. It matters to be less parochial. If ever there was a time, it is surely now" (Haraway 2014).

You don't know what is going to happen when you start to world your world with the worlds of those artists to whom you pay attention. You don't become like them, or, if you do, it is not personal. You follow their hands back to your own and only then realize that the hand from the Middle Ages is teaching your middle-aged hands how to stay present, how to start where you are, how to stay with the trouble, how to play with mystery. Sometimes very old hands can still teach you things you cannot predict. And sometimes, like all good teachers, they can simply point you to the teacher who's been patiently waiting for you to come inside and discover the world for yourself.

Note

1 Here you are alluding to some of the most influential theories of performance (especially the ontology of performance) over the last four decades. For performance and disappearance, see Phelan (1993); for performing remains, see Schneider (2011); for the restoration of behavior and repetition, see Schechner (1985); for performance, liveness, and mediation, see Auslander (1999), and for beyond repetition, see Colbert et al. (2020).

References

Abramović, Marina (2016), *Walk through Walls: A Memoir.* New York: Crown Archetype.
Adyashanti (2008), *The End of Your World.* Boulder, CO: Sounds True.
Af Klint, Hilma (2018), "Letters and Words Pertaining to Works by Hilma af Klint," in *Hilma af Klint: Notes and Methods*, Christine Burgin, ed., K. L. Bonnier and E. C. Wessel, translated from the Swedish, 246–85. Chicago: University of Chicago Press.
Allen, Theodore (1994), *The Invention of the White Race: Racial Oppression and Social Control*, vol. 1. London: Verso.
Aristotle, Leon Golden, and Hardison, O. B. (1990), *Aristotle's Poetics: A Translation and Commentary for Students of Literature.* Tallahassee: Florida State University Press.
Aronson-Lehavi, Sharon (2011), *Street Scenes: Late Medieval Acting and Performance (The New Middle Ages).* London: Palgrave Macmillan.
Artaud, Antonin (1958), *The Theatre and Its Double*, trans. Mary Caroline Richards. New York: Grove Press.
Aumiller, Rachel, ed. (2021), *A Touch of Doubt: On Haptic Scepticism.* Germany: De Gruyter.
Auslander, Philip (1999), "Live Performance in a Mediatized Culture," in *Liveness*, 10–60. London: Routledge.
Baert, Barbara (2011), *To Touch with the Gaze: Noli Me Tangere and the Iconic Space.* Gent: Iconology Research Group.
Bal, Mieke (1999), *Quoting Caravaggio: Contemporary Art, Preposterous History.* Chicago: University of Chicago Press.
Barnes, Jonathan, ed. (1984), *The Complete Works of Aristotle, the Revised Oxford Translation.* Princeton, NJ: Princeton University Press.
Bashkoff, Tracey (2018), "Paintings for the Temple," in *Hilma af Klint: Paintings for the Future*, Tracey Bashkoff, ed., 17–31. New York: Guggenheim Museum.
Baucom, Ian (2005), *Spectres of the Atlantic: Finance Capital, Slavery and the Philosophy of History.* Durham, NC: Duke University Press.

Bauman, Lynn, trans. (2003), *The Gospel of Thomas: Wisdom of the Twin*. Ashland, OR: White Cloud Press.

Beckett, Samuel (1954), *Waiting for Godot*. New York: Grove Press.

Bell, Rudolph M. (1985), *Holy Anorexia*. Chicago: University of Chicago Press.

Belting, Hans (1994), *Likeness and Presence: A History of the Image before the Era of Art*. Chicago: University of Chicago Press.

Benedict (1931), *Rule of Saint Benedict*, translated into English, *A Pax Book*, W.K. Lowther Clarke, preface. London: S.P.C.K.

Bilger, Burkhard (2016), "When Germans Make Peace with Their Dead," *New Yorker*, September 12, 2016, <https://www.newyorker.com/magazine/2016/09/12/familienaufstellung-germanys-group-therapy> accessed February 3, 2023.

Bochner, Mel (1967), *Artforum*, 6(4): 28–33.

Boss, Pauline (2000), *Ambiguous Loss: Learning to Live with Unresolved Grief*. Cambridge, MA: Harvard University Press.

Bourriaud, Nicholas (2002), *Relational aesthetics*. [Dijon]: Les Presses du réel.

Brecht, Bertolt (1961), "On Chinese Acting," trans. Eric Bentley, *TDR: The Drama Review*, 6(1): 130–6.

Brown, George MacKay (1989), *Portrait of Orkney*. London: John Murray Press.

Brown, Ivor (1926), *Masques and Phases*. London: Richard Cobden-Sanderson.

Bynum, Caroline Walker (1990), "Preface," in *Hildegard of Bingen: Scivias*, trans. Mother Columba Hard and Jane Bishop, 1–7. New York: Paulist Press.

Cabaud, Jacques (1964), *Simone Weil: A Fellowship in Love*. New York: Channel Press.

Carruthers, Mary and Ziolkowski, Jan M., eds (2002), *The Medieval Craft of Memory: An Anthology of Texts and Pictures*. Philadelphia: University of Pennsylvania Press.

Carson, Anne (2005), "Decreation: How Women Like Sappho, Marguerite Porete and Simone Weil Tell God," *Decreation: Poetry, Essays, Opera*, 156–83, New York: Vintage Books.

Cenere (Italy), Directed by Fabo Mari, Written by Fabo Mari and Eleonora Duse (Ambrosio Film Company, 1916), 38 min, <https://www.youtube.com/watch?v=op1X6P7e1BE> accessed February 2, 2023.

Chogyam Trungpa (2003), "Commentary," in *The Tibetan Book of the Dead: The Great Liberation through Hearing in the Bardo*, trans. Francesca Fremantle and Chogyam Trungpa, 1–45. Boston: Shambala.

Chogyam Trungpa (2008), *True Perception: The Path of Dharma Art*, ed. Judith Lief. Boston: Shambhala.

Colbert, S., Jones, D., and Vogel, S., eds (2020), *Race and Performance after Repetition*. Durham, NC: Duke University Press.

Coles, Robert (2001), *Simone Weil: A Modern Pilgrimage*. Woodstock, VT: Skylight Paths.

Coplans, John (1968), *Serial Imagery*. Pasadena Art Museum & New York Graphic Society.

Corbin, Henry (1975), "Mundus Imaginalis or the Imaginary and the Imaginal," https://www.amiscorbin.com/en/bibliography/mundus-imaginalis-or-the-imaginary-and-the-imaginal/ accessed February 1, 2023.

Creighton, Gilbert (1995), *Caravaggio and His Two Cardinals*. University Park: University of Pennsylvania Press.

Curtin, Adrian (2019), *Death in Modern Theatre: Stages of Mortality*. Manchester: Manchester University Press.

Danto, A., Iles, C., and Stokic, J. (2010), *Marina Abramović: The Artist Is Present*, ed. Klaus Biesenbach. New York: Museum of Modern Art.

Desikachar, T. K. V. (1995), *The Heart of Yoga: Developing a Personal Practice*. Rochester, VT: Inner Traditions International.

Didi-Huberman, Georges (1995), *Fra Angelico: Dissemblance and Figuration*, trans. Jane Marie Todd. Chicago: University of Chicago Press.

Didi-Huberman, Georges (2017), *The Surviving Image: Phantoms of Time and Time of Phantoms—Aby Warburg's History of Art*, trans. Harvey L. Mendelsohn. University Park, PA: Pennsylvania State University Press.

Douglass, Frederick ([1845] 1979), "The Cambria Riot, My Slave Experience, and My Irish Mission: An Address Delivered in Belfast, Ireland, on December 5, 1845," *Belfast Banner of Ulster*, December 9, 1845, and *Belfast Northern Whig*, December 9, 1845, in *The Frederick*

Douglass Papers: Series One—Speeches, Debates, and Interviews, ed. JohnBlassingame, 86. New Haven, CT: Yale University Press.

Douglass, Frederick (1950), *The Life and Writings of Frederick Douglass*, vol. 1, ed. Philip S. Foner. New York: International Publications.

"Drama" (Photocopy of an article from *The New Statesman* by Desmond McCarthy), June 16, 1928, GB 247 MS Gen 1659/401, Eleonora Duse Collection, University of Glasgow, Scotland.

"Duse in 'The Lady from the Sea'" (Photocopy of press cutting from *The Manchester Guardian*), June 8, 1923, GB 247 MS Gen 1659/134, Eleonora Duse Collection, University of Glasgow, Scotland.

"Duse Superb as Blind Wife in Tragic Drama" (George C. Warren, Photocopy of press cutting from [unidentified source]), March 14, 1924, GB 247 MS Gen 1659/160, Eleonora Duse Collection, University of Glasgow, Scotland.

"Eleanor [sic Eleonora] Duse without Artificial Glamour" (Photocopy of press cutting from *The New York Herald* [s.d.]), GB 247 MS Gen 1659/239, Eleonora Duse Collection, University of Glasgow, Scotland.

Fenton, Laurence (2014), "Frederick Douglass Aboard the Cambria," *History Ireland*, 22(5), https://www.historyireland.com/frederick-douglass-aboard-cambria-1845/ accessed June 20, 2023.

Forse, James (2002), "Religious Drama and Ecclesiastical Reform in the Tenth Century," *Early Theatre: A Journal Associated with the Records of Early English Drama*, 5(2): 47–70.

Fraser, Russell A. (1976), "Introduction: The English Drama from Its Beginnings to the Closing of the Theatres," in *Drama of the English Renaissance 1: The Tudor Period*, ed. Russell A. Fraser and Norman Rabkin, 1–19. New York: Macmillan.

Freud, S. (1914), "Remembering, Repeating and Working-Through (Further Recommendations on the Technique of Psycho-Analysis II)," The Standard Edition of the *Complete Psychological Works of Sigmund Freud*, 12: 145–56.

"Fuchs, Elinor (1933–)", *Contemporary Authors, New Revision Series*, <https://www.encyclopedia.com/arts/educational-magazines/fuchs-elinor-1933> accessed February 3, 2023.

Fuchs, Elinor (2004), "Visit to a Small Planet: Questions to Ask a Play," *Theatre* 34(2): 4–9.

Fuchs, Elinor (2007), "Waiting for Recognition: An Aristotle for Non-Aristotelean Drama," *Modern Drama* 50(4): 532–44.

Gilroy, Paul (1993), *The Black Atlantic: Modernity and Double Consciousness*. Cambridge, MA: Harvard University Press.

Goldman, Jonathan (1992), *Healing Sounds: The Power of Harmonics*. Rochester, VT: Healing Arts Press.

Gordon, Avery (1997), *Ghostly Matters: Haunting and the Sociological Imagination*. Minneapolis: University of Minnesota Press.

Gough, Kathleen M. (2014), *Kinship and Performance in the Black and Green Atlantic: Haptic Allegories*. London: Routledge.

Gough, Kathleen M. (2016), "Sole Histories: The Grammar of the Feet in Foot Washing for the Sole," in *It's All Allowed: The Performance Works of Adrian Howells*, ed. Deirdre Heddon and Dominic Johnson, 206–20. London: Live Art Development Agency & Intellect Books.

Gough, Kathleen M. (2020), "The Age of Duse: Notes for a Performative Lecture," *Imagined Theatres*,< https://imaginedtheatres.com/the-age-of-duse/> accessed June 20, 2023.

Halifax, Joan (2009), *Being with Dying: Cultivating Compassion and Fearlessness in the Presence of Death*. Boston: Shambhala.

Haraway, Donna (2014), "Anthropocene, Capitalocene, Chthulucene: Staying with the Trouble," http://opentranscripts.org/transcript/anthropocene-capitalocene-chthulucene/ accessed January 30, 2023.

Haraway, Donna (2016), *Staying with the Trouble: Making Kin in the Chthulucene*. Durham, NC: Duke University Press.

Hartman, Saidiya (1997), *Scenes of Subjection: Terror, Slavery, and Self-Making in Nineteenth-Century America*. Oxford: Oxford University Press.

Hegel, G. W. F. (1977), *Phenomenology of Spirit*, trans. A. V. Miller. Oxford: Clarendon Press.

Heidegger, Martin (1968), *What Is Called Thinking?* trans. J. Glenn Gray. New York: Harper Collins.

Hildegard of Bingen (1990), *Scivias*, trans. Mother Columba Hard and Jane Bishop. New York: Paulist Press.

Hillman, James (1998), *Healing Fiction*. Washington, DC: Spring.

Horowitz, David Max (2018), "'The World Keeps You in Fetters; Cast Them Aside': Hilma af Klint, Spiritualism, and Agency," in *Hilma af Klint: Paintings for the Future*, ed. Tracey Bashkoff, 128–33. New York: Guggenheim Museum.

Howells, Adrian (2011), "Interview with Adrian Howells," interview by Dan Prichard, of Balcony Productions, on behalf of the British Council, <https://vimeo.com/18162606> accessed February 8, 2023.

Ignatiev, Noel (1995), *How the Irish Became White*. London: Routledge.

James, C. L. R. (1938), *The Black Jacobins*. New York: Dial Press.

Jameson, Fredric (1998), *Brecht and Method*. London: Verso.

Justice, Alan D. (March 1979), "Trade Symbolism in the York Cycle," *Theatre Journal*, 31(1): 47–58.

Kubiak, Anthony (1991), "From Trope to Tragedy," in *Stages of Terror: Terrorism, Ideology, and Coercion as Theatre History*, 48–71. Bloomington: Indiana University Press.

Le Gallienne, Eva (1965), *Eleonora Duse: The Mystic in the Theatre*. Carbondale: Southern Illinois University Press.

Levi, Jacob (2021), "'Es wird Leib, es empfindet': Auto-Affection, Doubt, and the Philosopher's Hands," in *A Touch of Doubt: On Haptic Scepticism*, ed. RachelAumiller, 31–56. Germany: De Gruyter.

LeWitt, Sol (1967), "Paragraphs on Conceptual Art," *Artforum* 5(10): 79–83.

Lorca, Federico Garcia ([1933] 2010), "Theory and Play of the Duende," *in Search of Duende*, trans. Christopher Maurer, 56–72. New York: New Directions Books.

Lott, Eric (1995), *Love and Theft: Blackface Minstrelsy and the American Working Cass*. Oxford: Oxford University Press.

Mackey, Nathaniel (1978), "The Unruly Pivot: Wilson Harris' *The Eye of the Scarecrow*," *Texas Studies in Literature and Language* 20(4): 633–59.

Maddock, Fiona (2001), *Hildegard of Bingen: The Woman of Her Age*. London: Faber & Faber.

Meltzer, Francoise (2001), "The Hands of Simone Weil," *Critical Inquiry* 27(4): 611–28.

Menakem, Resmaa (2017), *My Grandmother's Hands: Racialized Trauma and the Pathways to Mending Our Hearts and Bodies*. Las Vegas: Central Recovery Press.

Moore, Thomas (2015), *A Religion of One's Own*. New York: Gotham Books.

Muller-Westermann, Iris (2018), "Introduction," in *Hilma af Klint: Notes and Methods*, ed. Christine Bergen, 7–13. Chicago: University of Chicago Press.

Nancy, Jean-Luc (1998), *Noli me tangere: On the Raising of the Body*, trans. Sarah Clift, Pascale-Anne Brault, and Michael Naas. New York: Fordham University Press.

Nelson, Peter (2011), "Seriality," *Architecture&* 3: 19–20.

Newman, Barbara (June 1985), "Hildegard of Bingen: Visions and Validation," *Church History* 54(2): 163–75.

Newman, Barbara (1990), "Introduction," in *Hildegard of Bingen: Scivias*, trans. Mother Columba Hard and Jane Bishop, 9–53. New York: Paulist Press.

Newman, Barbara (2021), *The Permeable Self: Five Medieval Relationships*. Philadelphia: University of Pennsylvania Press.

Noffke, Suzanne (2012), *Catherine of Siena: An Anthology*, 2 vols (Medieval and Renaissance Texts and Studies 406). Tempe: Arizona Center for Medieval and Renaissance Studies Press.

Pagani, Maria Pia (2017), "*Duende* Has No Age," in *Eleonora Duse and Cenere (Ashes): Centennial Essays*, ed. Maria Pia Pagani and Paul Fryer, 90–108. Jefferson, NC: McFarland.

Pagani, Maria Pia (2018), "An Actress-Manager for the Italian Film Industry in the 1910s," *Nineteenth Century Theatre and Film* 45(1): 81–95.

Patterson, Orlando (1982), *Slavery and Social Death: A Comparative Study*. Cambridge, MA: Harvard University Press.

Phelan, Peggy (1993), "The Ontology of Performance," *Unmarked*, 146–66. London: Routledge.

Pickering, Rachel, and Foster, Sally (2022), *Maeshowe and the Heart of Neolithic Orkney: Official Souvenir Guide*. Edinburgh: Historic Environment Scotland.

"Research-Creation" (n.d.), *The Pedagogical Impulse*, <https://thepedagogicalimpulse.com/research-methodologies/> accessed February 9, 2023.

Roberts, Margaret (1906), *Catherine of Siena and Her Times*. New York: G.P. Putnam's Sons.

Robertson, Elizabeth (2013), "*Noli me tangere:* The Enigma of Touch in Middle English Religious Literature and Art for and About Women," in *Reading Skin in Medieval Literature and Culture (The New Middle Ages)*, ed. Katie L. Walter, 29–55. London: Palgrave.

Robson, Mark (2019), *Theatre & Death*. London: Methuen Drama.

Salzberg, Sharon (2015), "Does Creativity Have to Come from Suffering?" <https://onbeing.org/blog/does-creativity-have-to-come-from-suffering/> accessed January 14, 2023.

Schechner, Richard (1985), "Restoration of Behavior," *Between Theatre and Anthropology*, 35–116. Philadelphia: University of Pennsylvania Press.

Schneider, Rebecca (2011), *Performing Remains: Art and War in Times of Theatrical Reenactment*. London: Routledge.

Schneider, Rebecca (2018), "That the Past May Yet Have Another Future: Gesture in the Times of Hands Up," *Theatre Journal* 70(3): 285–306.

Seay, Albert, and Tinctoris, Johannes (1965), "The Epositio Manus of Johannes Tinctoris," *Journal of Musical Theory* 9(2): 194–232.

Sheehy, Helen (2003), *Eleonora Duse: A Biography*. New York: Alfred A. Knopf.

Shore, Paul (January 1998), "The *Vita Christi* of Ludolph of Saxony and Its Influence on the *Spiritual Exercises* of Ignatius of Loyola," *Studies in the Spirituality of Jesuits* 30(1): 2–32.

Sica, Anna, and Wilson, Alison (2012), *The Murray Edwards Duse Collection*. Milano: Mimesis Edizioni.

"Simone Weil," *Stanford Encyclopedia of Philosophy*, <https://plato.stanford.edu/entries/simone-weil/> accessed February 3, 2023.

Skinner, Michael (2015), "Ancestral Ghosts in Your Genome," *TedXRainier* (January 5, 2015), <https://www.youtube.com/watch?v=f1Pf5S8Nbfk> accessed February 8, 2023.

Solnit, Rebecca (2014), *Men Explain Things to Me*. Chicago: Haymarket Books.

Solzhenitsyn, Aleksandr (1975), *The Gulag Archipelago 1918–1956: An Experiment in Literary Investigation*, vols 1–2, trans. Thomas P. Whitney. New York: Harper & Row.

Sontag, Susan (1963), "Simone Weil," *New York Review of Books* (February 1, 1963), <https://www.nybooks.com/articles/1963/02/01/simone-weil/> accessed February 3, 2023.

Spiller, Hortense (1987), "Mama's Baby, Papa's Maybe: An American Grammar Book," *Diacritics* 17(2): 64–81.

Springgay, S., and Truman, S. E. (2018), "On the Need for Methods Beyond Proceduralism: Speculative Middles, (In)tensions, and Response-Ability in Research," *Qualitative Inquiry* 24(3): 203–14.

Stanislavski, Konstantin ([1936] 2013), *An Actor Prepares*, trans. Elizabeth Reynolds Hapgood. London: Bloomsbury.

Stockhausen, Karlheinz (1959), "How Time Passes," *Die Reihe* 3: 10–40.

Sykora, Katharina (1983), *Das Phänomen Des Seriellen in Der Kunst: Aspekte Einer Künstlerischen Methode Von Monet Bis Zur Amerikanischen Pop Art*, Würzburg, Germany: Königshausen & T.J. Neumann.

Symons, Arthur (1927), *Eleonora Duse*. London: Benjamin Blom.

Twitchin, Mischa (2016), *The Theatre of Death: The Uncanny in Mimesis*. London: Palgrave.

Vacche, Angela Dalle (2008), *Diva: Defiance and Passion in Early Italian Cinema*. Austin: University of Texas Press.

Voss, Julia (2018), "The Traveling Hilma af Klint," in *Hilma af Klint: Paintings for the Future*, ed. Tracey Bashkoff, 49–63. New York: Guggenheim Museum.

Walsh, Milton (Spring 2011), "'To Always Be Thinking Somehow about Jesus': The Prologue of Ludolph's Vita Christi," *Studies in the Spirituality of the Jesuits* 43(1): 1–39.

Weaver, William (1984), *Duse: A Biography*. London: Thames & Hudson.

Weil, Simone (1952a), *Gravity and Grace*, ed. Gustave Thibon, trans. Arthur Wills. New York: G.P. Putnam's Sons.

Weil, Simone (1952b), *The Need for Roots: Prelude to a Declaration of Duties Toward Mankind*, trans. Arthur Wills. Boston: Beacon Press.

Weil, Simone (1957a), "Antigone," *Intimations of Christianity among the Ancient Greeks*, ed. and trans. Elisabeth Chase Geissbuhler, 18–23. London: Routledge & Kegan Paul.

Weil, Simone (1957b), "The Pythagorean Doctrine," in *Intimations of Christianity among the Ancient Greeks*, ed. and trans. Elisabeth Chase Geissbuhler, 151–202. London: Routledge & Kegan Paul.

Weil, Simone (1986), "Human Personality," in *Simone Weil: An Anthology*, ed. Sian Miles, 49–78. New York: Weidenfeld & Nicolson.

Weil, Simone (2009), *Waiting for God,* trans. Emma Craufurd. New York: Harper Perennial.

Wells-Barnett, Ida B. ([1892] 2002), *On Lynching*, intro. by Patricia Hill Collins. New York: Humanity Books.

Westcott, James (2010), *When Marina Abramović Dies: A Biography.* Cambridge, MA: MIT Press.

Williams, Eric (1944), *Capitalism and Slavery.* Chapel Hill: University of North Carolina Press.

Williams, Patricia (1992), *The Alchemy of Race and Rights.* Cambridge, MA: Harvard University Press.

Wolynn, Mark (2016), *It Didn't Start with You: How Inherited Family Trauma Shapes Who We Are and How to End the Cycle.* New York: Penguin.

Young, Harvey (2010), *Embodying Black Experience.* Ann Arbor: University of Michigan Press.

Index

Note: Page numbers followed by n. and number represent endnotes and note number respectively.

Abramović, Marina 5, 113 n.5, 114–15 n.10, 129 n.3, 134, 154
  The Life 105, 114 n.6
  The Life and Death of Marina Abramovic (Wilson) 104, 107, 113 n.5
  "Relation Works" 7
  Rhythm 0 (1974) 115 n.10
  Rhythm 2 (1974) 115 n.10
  Rhythm 4 (1974) 114 n.10
  Rhythm 5 (1973) 114 n.10
  Rhythm 10 (1973) 19, 23–4, 108–13
  Walk through Walls 103–4
acting/actor 23–4, 75, 88, 97–115
  medieval 101, 103, 111
  modern 61, 63, 68
  in mystery play 97
  pain and 100, 101
  students 21, 61
  teacher 61–3, 77 n.2
  training 21–2, 63–4
  theory 23
  An Actor Prepares (Stanislavski) 21, 61–2
Adler, Stella 77 n.2
Adyashanti
  The End of Your World 149–50
af Klint, Hilma 5–6, 7, 19–20, 25–6, 131–147
  early career 139–40
  Hilma af Klint: A Pioneer of Abstraction (Moderna Museet, Stockholm) 143
  Hilma af Klint: Paintings for the Future (Guggenheim Museum, New York) 7, 25, 133, 143

Hilma af Klint: Painting the Unseen (Serpentine Gallery, London) 143
  midlife career 140–3
  Paintings for the Temple 133–4, 135–6, 146 n.1
  The Ten Largest 20, 25, 135–6, 145
  vision of the world 143–6
afterlife 22, 65–7, 77
Afterlife Awareness Conference, Orlando, Florida 7, 22, 66–7
The Alchemy of Race and Rights (Williams) 118
alienation 22–3, 81, 125, 128
alienation effect 22–3, 75–7, 81, 88
ambiguous loss 87, 96 n.8
Angel 1, 2, 50, 132
Annunciation 39, 82
  of Hildegard of Bingen 38–43
"Antigone" (Weil) 82, 84
Aristotle 30, 31, 34, 93 n.1
  De Anima 18–19
  Poetics 20, 29
Artaud, Antonin
  The Theatre and Its Double 24, 122–4
Assisi 5, 53, 78 n.5, 81, 82, 94 n.3
Aumiller, Rachel 12

Bardo 88, 120
  gap and 8, 89, 90, 125, 126, 128, 129, 149
Barnhouse stone 4
Beckett, Samuel
  Waiting for Godot 1, 87
Bell, Rudolph M. 85
Belting, Hans 77 n.3

Benedictine 5, 7, 20, 34, 38, 42, 43 n.1, 43 n.2, 44 n.5, 44 n.7
Between Ourselves (magazine) 84
Bochner, Mel 14
Boss, Pauline 95 n.8
Bourriaud, Nicholas 12
Brecht, Bertolt
  alienation effect 22–3, 75–7, 81, 88
Brown, George MacKay
  Portrait of Orkney 4
Buddha 55, 57, 78 n.5
Buddhists 10, 33, 55, 137, 156
burial chamber
  Maeshowe, Orkney Islands 2–4

The Cambria (ship) 24, 119, 124, 129 n.2
Camus, Albert 5, 83
Caravaggio 126–9, 132
  The Incredulity of Saint Thomas 25, 126–7
Carruthers, Mary
  The Medieval Craft of Memory 16, 151–2
Catherine of Siena 85–6, 89, 95 n.6
Cenere (Ashes) 22, 69, 70, 71, 72, 75, 76–7, 78 n.6, 79
character 20, 29–34, 41, 42, 48, 66, 70, 74, 75, 76, 87, 88, 97, 99, 111, 117, 125
  discipline and 33–7
  pain and 100–1
Charlemagne 49
Christian Mass 1, 48, 49
Chogyam Trungpa 88, 137–9
  The Tibetan Book of the Dead 88
  True Perception: The Path of Dharma Art 137
Coles, Robert 94 n.4
Coplans, John 14
Corbin, Henry 39–40
Covid-19 pandemic
  theory of ambiguous loss 95 n.8

"The Creative Journey: Artists in Conversation with the Dalai Lama on Spirituality and Creativity" 155–6
Crucifixion 22, 71, 93 n.1, 102, 103
  and Crucifixion complex 101, 103
The Crucifixion (play) 98–100
Curtin, Adrian
  Death in Modern Theatre 9

De Anima (Aristotle) 18–19
death 1, 4, 7, 9, 88, 95 n.5
  definitions 9
  dramatization of Christ 22, 23, 49–50, 52, 59 n.4
  in form of impermanence 10, 11, 157
  Marina Abramović and 103–8, 113–14 n.5, 115 n.10
  Hilma af Klint and 132, 134, 135, 143
  Eleonora Duse and 67, 69–73, 76–7
  Hildegard of Bingen and 34, 42
  Simone Weil and 7, 22, 82, 83–6
  resurrection 51
  symbolic 38
Death in Modern Theatre (Curtin) 9
Deledda, Grazia 70, 78 n.5
Department of Theatre, University of Vermont 6–7
Descent from the Cross (Duccio) 69–72
Didi-Huberman, Georges 58 n.3, 78 n.4
discipline 6, 9, 12, 14, 47, 156
  artistic 15, 26
  and character 33–7
  defined 34
  fasting and physical 95 n.6
doubles, theatre 24–5, 97, 98, 103, 112, 121, 124, 125, 128
  The Theatre and Its Double (Artaud) 122–4

Doubting Thomas 25, 125
Douglass, Frederick 24, 119, 120, 124, 129 n.1, 129, n.2
dramaturgy 13, 15–16, 26, 79
  and dramaturge 4
Duccio
  Descent from the Cross 69–72
duende 25–6, 69, 80 n.7, 131–33, 144
Duse, Eleonora 5, 7, 19, 21–2, 63. *See also Cenere (Ashes)*
  archive 63, 77 n.1, 82
  death 70
  life 67–77
  plaster cast of hand 64–5
  role as director 76
dying 7, 10, 12, 22, 42, 67, 82, 86, 87, 109, 156. *See also* death
The Dying Arts 9, 12–15

Earl Harald Maddadarson 3
Easter Mass 1, 2
education, and healing 11–12, 27 n.4
eighth climate (imaginal world)
  Hildegard of Bingen and 40
  Sufism and 40, 53
Eliot, T. S. 83
Encyclopedia Britannica 9
end-of-life doula 7, 10, 22, 86
The End of Your World (Adyashanti) 149–50
Europe 24, 27 n.2, 38, 49, 50, 118–19
  burial chamber in 2
  medieval 69
Expositio manus (Tinctoris) 18, 154

The Five (De Fem) 134–5, 146
Foot Washing for the Sole (Howells) 101, 102
Forse, James 27 n.2
Fra Angelico 52, 55, 58 n.3
Free French 95 n.5
Fuchs, Elinor 81, 87, 157
  "Visit to a Small Planet: Questions to Ask a Play" 156–7

genre 15, 21, 43 n.3, 47–8, 51, 122–3, 127–8
gesture 21–2, 58, 61, 63, 65, 75
gestus (social) 75–6
Giotto di Bondone 53
  Lamentation 69, 70, 71
  Scenes from the Life of Mary Magdalen 53
Goldman, Jonathan 44 n.7
  Healing Sounds: The Power of Harmonics 44 n.7
Gough, Kathleen
  Kinship and Performance in the Black and Green Atlantic 24, 119–20
Gough, Thomas 24–5, 124
Gough, William 119
Green Tara 55, 56
Gregorian chant 32, 33, 39, 44 n.7
grief 21, 27 n.4, 51, 87
Guggenheim Museum 7, 25, 133, 143, 145
Guidonian Hand 16–20, 26, 151–4
Guido of Arezzo 16, 151

Halifax, Joan 10
hand(s) 16, 18, 19, 20–2, 25, 26, 61, 62, 150–4, 156, 158
  Caravaggio and 126–9
  Eleonora Duse and 63–5, 67, 68, 69, 75, 76
  Guidonian Hand 16–20, 26, 151–4, 158
  Hildegard of Bingen and 35–6
  Hilma af Klint and 25, 146
  Jesus's 22
  Marina Abramović and 109, 111, 112, 117
  My Grandmother's Hands (Menakem) 19, 24, 117–18
  Noli me tangere and 51–8, 58 n.4
  plaster cast(s) 19, 22, 64–5, 68, 76, 89

Pythagoras and 90–3
Simone Weil and 81, 87, 89–90
stagehands 150
"The Hands of Simone Weil"
   (Meltzer) 89–90
Haraway, Donna 157
healing, education and 11–12, 27 n.4
Healing Fiction (Hillman) 15
*Healing Sounds: The Power of
   Harmonics* (Goldman) 44 n.7
Hegel, G. W. F. 19
Hildegard of Bingen 5, 7, 19, 20, 26,
   32, 34–7, 43 n.4
   Annunciation of 38–43
   Ordo Virtutum 42, 43 n.3
   Scivias 36
   Symphonia 43 n.3
Hillman, James 106
   Healing Fiction 15
*Hilma af Klint: A Pioneer of
   Abstraction* (Moderna
   Museet, Stockholm) 143
*Hilma af Klint: Paintings for the
   Future* (Guggenheim
   Museum, New York) 7, 25,
   133, 143
*Hilma af Klint: Painting the
   Unseen* (Serpentine Gallery,
   London) 143
Holy Anorexia (Bell) 85
hospice 7, 10, 11, 66, 67, 86
Howells, Adrian
   Foot Washing for the Sole 101, 102

Ignatius of Loyola 74
imaginal world (Corbin) 40, 62, 66.
   See also *mundus imaginalis*
impermanence 10, 11, 157
The Incredulity of Saint Thomas
   (Caravaggio) 25, 126–7
invisible world 16, 139, 141, 144,
   152, 155
*It Didn't Start with You: How
   Inherited Family Trauma
   Shapes Who We Are and
   How to End the Cycle*
   (Wolynn) 104

Jameson, Fredric 75–6
Jesus 1, 21, 22, 51–2, 55, 57–9, 62, 63,
   69–71, 74, 76, 97–103, 124–8,
   129 n.4, 143

*Kinship and Performance in the
   Black and Green Atlantic*
   (Gough) 24, 119–20
knowledge 6, 141
   conceptual 11
   embodied experience and 11, 12,
      66, 74, 94 n.3, 118, 123, 142
   skepticism and 12
   sensual 59 n.4
Kubiak, Anthony 93 n.1

Lamentation (Giotto) 69, 70,
   71
La Porta Chiusa (The Closed Door)
   (Praga, Marco) 70
La Porziuncola 81, 82
The Last Judgement (play) 26, 26 n.1,
   97, 149
Last Supper 98, 101, 102
Law of Octaves 43 n.2
Le Gallienne, Eva
   Mystic in the Theatre 78 n.5
Legenda (Raymond of Capua) 95 n.7
Lehman Master 52, 54
LeWitt, Sol 14, 15
The Life (Abramovic) 105, 114 n.6
*The Life and Death of Marina
   Abramovic* (Wilson) 104, 107,
   113 n.5
Live Art Development Agency,
   London 7
Lorca, Federico Garcia 69, 80 n.7,
   131, 132, 144
   "Theory and Play of the Duende"
      80 n.7, 131, 144

Los Angeles County Museum of Art 143, 147 n.2
loyalty, unconscious 106
Ludolph of Saxony 73–4

Maddadarson, Harald 2, 3, 27 n.3
Maeshowe (Orkney Islands) 2–4
Magdalene, Mary 21, 22, 51–8, 59 n.4, 131, 143, 154
Magnus, Albertus 58 n.3
Marys (the three) 1, 2, 3, 49, 50, 69
Medicine Buddha 55, 57
medieval art 69, 86, 131
The Medieval Craft of Memory (Carruthers and Ziolkowski) 16, 151–2
medieval pedagogy 8
medieval relationships 8–9
meditation 7, 17, 44 n.7, 73–4, 155
   silent retreat 7, 33, 67
medium 18, 22, 29, 51, 65, 66, 67, 69, 75, 77, 139, 140
Meisner, Sanford 77 n.2
Meltzer, Francoise 19, 89–90
Menakem, Resmaa 19, 24, 117, 118–19
   My Grandmother's Hands 19, 24, 117–18
Men Explain Things to Me (Solnit) 44 n.6
metaxu 90
Middle Ages 1, 5, 15, 16, 119, 153
Moderna Museet in Stockholm 143
Monastery of the Immaculate Heart of Mary 38, 44 n.5
Monk, Meredith
   Monk and the Abbess 43 n.3
Moore, Thomas 83
   A Religion of One's Own 81
morality play 42
Mother Earth 2
mundus imaginalis (Corbin) 39–40
musical thinking 43 n.2. *See also* Law of Octaves

My Grandmother's Hands (Menakem) 19, 24, 117–18
mystery 5, 21, 26 n.1, 43, 47
   defined 47, 103
   esoteric 6
   medieval 5
mystery play (medieval) 1, 5, 6, 8, 13, 16, 21, 23, 25, 26, 26 n.1, 48, 81, 97–8, 102, 149, 155
   actors in 97–103
   "a visit to a tomb" (Visitatio Sepulchri) 1–2, 27 n.2, 49
mystic 5, 32, 43 n.3–4, 65, 66, 67, 133
Mystic in the Theatre (Le Gallienne) 78 n.5
mysticism 35, 78 n.5

Nancy, Jean-Luc 58 n.4
The Need for Roots (Weil) 95 n.5
Nelson, Peter 15
Neolithic 2, 3, 4
Newman, Barbara 16, 72, 75
   The Permeable Self: Five Medieval Relationships 8
Noah's Ark 98
Noli me tangere 19, 21, 51, 54, 55, 58 n.3, 58 n.4, 89
Norse 2, 3
North Sea 2

Odette (play) 79 n.6
"On Being" blog (Salzberg) 155
Ordo Virtutum (Hildegard) 42, 43 n.3
Orkney Islands
   Maeshowe (Neolithic burial chamber) 2–4
Orlando, Florida
   Afterlife Awareness Conference 7

Paintings for the Temple (af Klint) 133–4, 135–6, 146 n.1
Papini, Giorgio 22, 69, 76, 79 n.6
pedagogy 8, 11, 12, 16

performance artists 100, 104
permeable self 8, 11, 16, 72, 75
The Permeable Self: Five Medieval Relationships (Newman) 8
Perrin, J. M. 94 n.3
personas 30, 31
personhood 8, 71, 72
Plato
　Symposium 90
Poetics (Aristotle) 20, 29
Portrait of Orkney (Brown) 4
Porziuncola, Assisi 5
Praga, Marco
　La Porta Chiusa (*The Closed Door*) 70
Pythagoras 23, 82, 85, 90–3, 134
"The Pythagorean Doctrine" (Weil) 82

Quem quaeritis ("whom do you seek?") 2, 21, 27 n.2, 49, 81

race 24, 117–21, 124, 129 n.1
Raymond of Capua
　Legenda 95 n.7
realism 24, 122, 123, 124, 125, 127, 128
relation/s 3, 4, 9, 10, 13, 15, 16, 18, 19, 20, 82, 83, 86, 106, 122, 124, 154, 155, 157
　relational 6, 9, 20, 29, 96 n.7, 106, 128
　relational art 12
　relationality 14, 128
　relatable 5, 11
relationships
　between education and healing 11–12, 27 n.4
　hands and 19, 61
　mathematical 89–90
　medieval pedagogical 8–9
　series and 13, 14, 15
　Simone Weil and 83, 85, 86, 88, 95 n.7

"Relation Works" (Abramović) 7
A Religion of One's Own (Moore) 81
religious icons 65, 77 n.3
research-creation 13–14
Rhythm 0 (Abramović) 115 n.10
Rhythm 2 (Abramović) 115 n.10
Rhythm 4 (Abramović) 114 n.10
Rhythm 5 (Abramović) 114 n.10
Rhythm 10 (Abramović) 19, 23–4, 108–13
"Rhythms" (1973–4) 114–15 n.10
Ring of Brodgar 2
Robertson, Elizabeth 59 n.4
Robson, Mark 9
Rule of St. Benedict 34, 37, 39

Salzberg, Sharon 155
Scenes from the Life of Mary Magdalen (Giotto) 53
scepticism 12 *See also* skepticism
　doubt and 12, 25, 35, 125, 127, 129
Schneider, Rebecca 4–5, 10, 19
　"That the Past May Yet Have Another Future" 4
Scivias (Hildegard) 36
serial
　art 14, 15
　method 14, 15
　order 14, 140
　structure 14
　thinking 141
Serial Imagery (Coplans) 14
seriality 14, 15
series 6, 9, 10, 12, 13, 14, 15, 16, 19, 20, 25, 26, 89, 102, 113 n.1, 113 n.5, 114 n.10, 127, 135, 137, 138, 139, 140, 145, 147 n.1, 149, 153, 156
Serpentine Gallery, London 105, 106, 114 n.6, 136, 143
silence 4, 5, 39, 68, 79
silent medium 69, 75
skepticism
　knowledge and 12

doubt and 12, 25, 35, 125, 127, 129
slavery 24, 118–121, 124, 129 n.1, 129 n.2
social gestus (Brecht) 75
Solesmes Congregation 43 n.5
Solnit, Rebecca
   Men Explain Things to Me 44 n.6
Solzhenitsyn, Aleksandr 120
Sontag, Susan 85
sound 18, 40, 44 n.7, 51, 109, 111
sound healing 7, 41, 44 n.7
The Spiritual in Art: Abstract Painting 1890 (Los Angeles County Museum of Art) 147 n.2
Springgay, S. 11, 13
Stanislavski, Konstantin 21, 22, 61, 62, 63, 77 n.2
   An Actor Prepares 21, 61–2
   actor training 63–4
   theory of building character 74
Strasberg, Lee 77 n.2
Sufis 39, 40, 42, 53
sui generis 154
survivals 65, 78 n.4
The Surviving Image: Phantoms of Time and Time of Phantoms—Aby Warburg's History of Art (Didi-Huberman) 78 n.4
Sykora, Katharina 14
Symphonia (Hildegard) 43 n.3
Symposium (Plato) 90

The Ten Largest (af Klint) 20, 25, 135–6, 145
"That the Past May Yet Have Another Future" (Schneider) 4
theater of cruelty (Artaud) 123–4
Theater of Death: The Uncanny in Mimesis (Twitchin) 10
The Theatre and Its Double (Artaud) 24, 122–4
Theatre & Death (Robson) 9

Theatron 26, 149–58
"Theory and Play of the Duende" (Lorca) 80 n.7, 131, 144
Thibon, Gustave 94 n.3
Thomas (biblical) 24–5, 120, 124, 125, 126–7, 128–9, 143
The Tibetan Book of the Dead (Chogyam Trungpa) 88
Tinctoris, Johannes
   Expositio manus 18, 154
transgenerational trauma 7, 19, 23–5, 117–24, 138
trauma 7, 19, 23–5, 104, 106, 109, 111, 112, 117–24, 138
treatise on the hand/treatise on synesthesia 18–19
True Perception: The Path of Dharma Art (Chogyam Trungpa) 137
Truman, S. E. 11, 13
Twitchin, Mischa
   Theater of Death: The Uncanny in Mimesis 10

unconscious loyalty 106
University of Glasgow 7, 22
University of Vermont (UVM) Department of Theatre 6–7

Vermont 7, 41
vinyasa krama (wise progression) 14–15
Visitatio Sepulchri ("a visit to a tomb") 1–2, 27 n.2, 49
   burial chamber 1–4
"Visit to a Small Planet: Questions to Ask a Play" (Fuchs) 156–7
Vita Christi (Ludolph of Saxony) 73–4
Volmar 42

Waiting for God (Weil) 94 n.3
Waiting for Godot (Beckett) 1, 87
Walk through Walls (Abramović) 103–4

Warburg, Aby 78 n.4
Ward, Chip 44 n.6
Weaver, William 78 n.5
Weil, Simone 5, 7, 19, 22, 23, 81, 82, 93 n.2
  "Antigone" 82, 84
  birth 84
  death 83–4, 88–9
  hands 89–90
  The Need for Roots 95 n.5
  "The Pythagorean Doctrine" 82
  relationships 83–92
  Waiting for God 94 n.3
Wells, Ida B. 119
Williams, Patricia
  The Alchemy of Race and Rights 118
Wilson, Robert
  The Life and Death of Marina Abramovic 104, 107, 113 n.5
wisdom 8, 11, 125, 129, 157
Wolynn, Mark
  It Didn't Start with You: How Inherited Family Trauma Shapes Who We Are and How to End the Cycle 104

yoga 14–15
Yoga Sutra 15

Zen koan 17, 125
Ziolkowski, Jan M.
  The Medieval Craft of Memory 16, 151–2

www.ingramcontent.com/pod-product-compliance
Lightning Source LLC
Chambersburg PA
CBHW052122300426
44116CB00010B/1767